Solving the Reading Riddle

The Librarian's Guide to Reading Instruction

Rita Soltan

LIBRARIES UNLIMITED

AN IMPRINT OF ABC-CLIO, LLC
Santa Barbara, California • Denver, Colorado • Oxford, England

Copyright 2010 by ABC-CLIO, LLC

Library of Congress Cataloging-in-Publication Data

Soltan, Rita.
   Solving the reading riddle : the librarian's guide to reading instruction / Rita Soltan.
       p. cm.
   Includes bibliographical references and index.
   ISBN 978-1-59158-844-3 (acid-free paper) — ISBN 978-1-59158-843-6 (ebook)
   1. Libraries and new literates. 2. Literacy programs. 3. Family literacy programs. 4. Children's librarians—Professional relationships. 5. School librarian participation in curriculum planning. 6. Reading. 7. Reading—History. I. Title.
   Z716.45.S65 2010
   027.6—dc22   2010000292

ISBN: 978-1-59158-844-3
E-ISBN: 978-1-59158-843-6

14   13   12   11   10   1   2   3   4   5

This book is also available on the World Wide Web as an e-book.
Visit http://www.abc-clio.com for details.

Libraries Unlimited
An Imprint of ABC-CLIO, LLC

ABC-CLIO, LLC
130 Cremona Drive, P.O. Box 1911
Santa Barbara, California 93116-1911

This book is printed on acid-free paper ∞

Manufactured in the United States of America

For Joshua and Asher
May you always love to read

Contents

Preface: Navigating the Labyrinth of Reading Instruction

My thirty-year career as a public children's librarian placed me in the world of children's reading with a focus and goals parallel to those of the teacher or reading specialist. Connecting children with books through readers' advisory rather than reading instruction was my primary role, while creating programs, story hours, summer reading plans, and book discussion series all had the underlying purpose of encouraging kids, as much as possible, not only to read but *to like reading*. I immersed myself in the plethora of children's literature in all genres, including nonfiction formats, ready to deal with each "reference interview." Over the years, I worked in well-endowed upper-middle-class communities and underfunded urban neighborhoods where, for most kids, life is a daily ordeal of poverty and, often, family illiteracy. I provided hundreds of books to thousands of children, first and foremost, for homework assignments, book reports, and research projects. The children that truly loved to come and visit with me were those I got to know for their avid attitude and eagerness to read regardless of where they lived. Matching these children with the right book was always a satisfying pleasure. However, finding the right fit for the uninterested or struggling reader was much more difficult.

Each library or community I worked in, whether affluent or underprivileged, had an approach to reading instruction—sometimes an old established approach, and sometimes a newly innovative one. Children came to the library with all kinds of restrictions or requirements based on how each assignment/book report needed to be fulfilled. As the years progressed, I watched the philosophy and methodology used to teach these children reading as it was constantly interpreted and instituted by researchers, administrators, and politicians—then altered with aims for improvement. I heard the terms "phonics instruction," "whole language," and "basal readers" at PTA meetings and faculty sessions I attended to promote the library. I had a vague understanding of what all these terms implied, but never really comprehended why some approaches worked over others and why, with all the research-based theories, children still struggled to read, became discouraged, and even became uninterested in reading and in learning.

In recent years, I became intrigued again by the methods of reading instruction as I observed my daughter, a newly minted teacher and reading specialist, incorporate what she explained was a balanced literacy curriculum in her K–2 classrooms. And then, through my volunteer efforts at my local elementary school, I was introduced to "Reading Recovery" and a barrage of "little leveled books" that encompassed a literacy library. I was simultaneously fascinated and aghast at how these very basic, very controlled books were being used to provide successful intervention for children who were not gaining literacy skills in their regular classroom. Fascinated by how some of these slower learners were achieving, while aghast at how, despite the stunted, boring, and repetitive language used in the texts, these little books were well-received and seemed to successfully compete with the carefully and beautifully designed easy- and beginning-reader books available in the trade market.

I am convinced that if, as public youth services librarians, readers' advisory and to a broader extent, reference services, remains our primary focus, it is important to assess and understand reading instruction. Over the last seventy-five years, the various types of reading materials and programs developed for reading instruction have evolved, changed, and reemerged. The "reading wars" dilemma or argument has become not only a political football, but a confusing mix of theories for those outside the pedagogical community. Programs, from the traditional "Dick and Jane" whole-word method, to the phonics-based or alphabetic principle, to whole language using trade books such as the land-mark Harper & Row "I Can Read Series," to today's "leveled texts and little books" pioneered in New Zealand's Reading Re-covery intervention, are all examples of the diversity of methods being used to teach children to read.

As youth librarians, it behooves us to review the history of reading instruction over the last several decades to help us understand how methods and philosophies developed, changed, and are being used today. This background knowledge provides insight into how we can address the various roles we play through the service we provide with a commitment to a com-munity's literacy efforts. Keeping up with today's various reading curriculums, and there are numerous to be sure, solidifies our professional connections and responsibilities and provides bal-ance to the community's educational needs.

Acknowledgments

My journey in writing this book began in the Educational Resources Laboratory at Oakland University in Rochester, Michigan, where, following a long career as a public children's librarian, I began working part-time as a cataloger. Surrounded by education professors and a collection devoted to instruction, in particular, the myriad possibilities for teaching reading, I made a bold decision to go back to school in mid-life to learn about reading from another perspective. What I discovered led me to realize how I wanted to share my newly acquired insight with my library colleagues. I am particularly grateful for the invaluable knowledge and wisdom I gained from two wonderful mentors. Dr. Annette Osborne was more than willing to share her graduate level children's literature classroom and her love of particular authors and titles through a co-teaching arrangement we created. I want to thank her for her willingness, encouragement, and patience. Bobbi Amigh introduced me to the power of Reading Recovery, literacy libraries, and early intervention. Her positive, upbeat disposition always made the children and me feel special and productive. To my long-time friend and colleague, Jane Kahan, I say thank you for reading a very early draft and letting me know that I was making sense. I want to also thank my editor Barbara Ittner, whose guidance and clear direction helped me to mold this book into a handbook for librarians both in and out of the school setting. Lastly, my admiration and love goes to my daughter Eva, a superb teacher, reading tutor, and mother.

Introduction

I was visiting one of my colleagues at her library one afternoon, shortly before the end of the school year, when she took out a brochure from the local school district advertising the district's upcoming "Super Summer Success" reading program. Examining it closely, I immediately realized that the program was designed around a specific reading curriculum aimed to encourage at-risk children to continue reading at their own "independent reading level" while simultaneously catering to their interests throughout the summer. The detailed Web site created for parents and teachers included a plethora of well-designed information, complete with resources for purchasing and locating the correct books and titles for the program. These resources included book distributors, literacy organizations such as Reading Is Fundamental (RIF), online bookstores, and brick-and-mortar local establishments. Book bags for summer checkout were to be created for each participating child and would include six "leveled" books, bookmarks, and a program explanation sheet. Participating children were allowed to select their own books from a preselected collection of leveled titles. Throughout the information presented to both parents and educators, the one thing missing, which my friend was quite disturbed by, was the fact that nowhere was there any mention of visiting a library as a component of this program. The public library was ignored in both the planning and implementation of this worthwhile effort aimed at reducing summer reading achievement loss. What was happening here in a county with numerous well-maintained and generously funded public libraries? I believe there was a lack of understanding in terms of what the district viewed as effective continued reading instruction and what the public library staff knew about how reading instruction is offered today. Both sides were correct, yet needed to communicate more effectively to each other. The district wished to maintain reading at the "independent level" for each at-risk child by providing books from their successful literacy collections, while the library staff knew it could provide an extension of the program through its collections and summer reading programming. The missing key to the communication was acknowledgement and understanding from both sides of reading instruction practice and philosophy. The library staff did not quite know the meaning of "independent reading level" in terms of reading instruction, while the district staff felt compelled to assure success through their established reading curriculum and literacy collection. This encounter with my colleague and friend made me think about why children's librarians need a guide to today's reading instruction in order to provide enhanced services to their communities.

While reading instruction has been in the forefront of educational news in both good and bad reports, the instructional methods have been a source of confusion for most people not immediately immersed in the context of teaching. Reading scores and phonics versus whole language come to mind when reading instruction is considered, but the underlying principles, strategies, and goals of reading instruction are vague concepts to most far from the everyday life of today's classroom teacher. Children's librarians are wonderful experts in promoting reading through literature and programming, but the actual basics and mechanics of teaching reading are often non-defined or unspecified. This book intends to make reading instruction and its various methods clearer, so that you, as a librarian, can use the added knowledge to strengthen the various roles you play in your professional career. Ultimately, it is hoped that integrating this new knowledge into your overall understanding and daily practice results in more and better readers.

The book is divided into two parts, with chapters within each.

Part 1

"Everything Old is New Again" includes three chapters on the nuts and bolts of reading instruction. In reviewing a history of the last seventy-five years, it is evident that many of the approaches and practices have not actually changed, but have evolved into similar philosophies with new terminology.

Chapter 1

"Historical Overview" recounts how reading instruction developed, with an emphasis on the Dick and Jane Look-See method, the alphabetic principle behind phonics, the introduction of basal readers, followed by the whole language philosophy culminating in today's balanced literacy environment.

Chapter 2

"New Approaches for the Struggling Reader" focuses on methods used with children who fall behind or through the cracks and explains how today's varied approaches including the New Zealand pioneered Reading Recovery program and the numerous offshoots that include leveled literacy classroom libraries are making successful interventions.

Chapter 3

"What It All Means Today" puts the preceding information in perspective in terms of what is happening in today's classrooms and describes the specifics of how children are tested, evaluated, and taught to read, along with explanations of today's teaching terminology.

Part 2

"The Reading Riddle and the Role of the Children's Librarian—Dovetailing Roles with Reading Instruction" covers youth services in terms of today's reading instructional approaches and philosophy within four defined roles, each covered in a separate chapter. It also addresses how knowledge of reading instruction can dovetail with library youth services and throughout the residential, business, and educational communities.

Chapter 4

"The Reading Advocate" looks into the primary role of advocacy in terms of readers' advisory and reference service. Children's librarians can incorporate common reading instruction principles with their day-to-day advisory services and programming schedules to provide service with a more cognizant approach.

Chapter 5

"Family Reading Coach" considers the family as the most important and initial source of literacy instruction and how librarians act as coaches to encourage reading in the home.

Chapter 6

"Partner with Educators" aims to foster new approaches for collaboration between school and library personnel and encourages librarians to extend this collaboration throughout the educational community by participation in one or more communities of practice, a less formal, social-oriented form of networking and sharing of resources.

Chapter 7

"Keeper of the Tools" stresses access to reading and reading opportunities beyond classic collection-development initiatives through the concepts of visibility, compatibility, and portability of supporting reading and literacy materials with special attention to today's goals for reading instruction.

Chapter 8

"Insights" concludes with some overall observations of what the past seventy-five years of reading instruction has meant to readers, and how we as children's librarians are a crucial part of the developing philosophy and strategy. "Keeping up with Trends" is an annotated list of teaching and reading instruction resources.

Finally, a "Glossary of Reading Instruction Terminology" provides definitions for some of the pedagogical lingo floating around today's literacy community.

To try to solve the reading riddle, it is important to evaluate how reading instruction has impacted education as a whole and how evaluating it from different directions can reflect on your perceptive knowledge as a children's librarian.

PART 1

Everything Old Is New Again

Exploring and evaluating the history of reading instruction reveals a surprising cycle of former methods and philosophies resurfacing as newer concepts with modern terminology.

CHAPTER 1

Reading History

On the first night of the first graduate level reading course I enrolled in, the professor began with an exercise that involves reading a story called "The Sam Trap: A Primer in Applebet" (May 1982, 12). The story is presented with a series of symbols, much like hieroglyphs, to gain access to a reading code. A glossary of symbols is provided, and as the sentences become increasingly longer and more complicated, so too does the reading difficulty. Along with the other education students, I struggled to remember which squiggle and which version of a line symbol represented each letter in the words and passages. The professor's point in this exercise was clear. Like learning a foreign language with a different alphabetic code such as Hebrew, Greek, or Russian, the symbols that make up our English language can be just as daunting and confusing when first approached by a new reader.

The scribes of Mesopotamia were at once writers and readers, interpreting the symbols, phonetic representations, words, and eventual meaning of the text they created for basic written communication. From these early days, reading instruction developed as a skills-based, symbol-oriented practice. Cuneiform writing using symbols to represent specific sounds was the forerunner of a letter-level method representing phonetic sounds for each individual letter/symbol and combination thereof for meaningful words. From this system, short sentences were devised with the intention of transmitting a purposeful message that, in turn, led to the recording of complex and sophisticated, literature, history, and scientific knowledge.

Similar patterns are evident in the various methods employed over a four-century period of American reading instruction. In colonial America, the Alphabet Method taught children to identify the letters orally and then recite combinations of letters with their corresponding sounds. These "nonsense syllables" expanded to simple, one-syllable words, followed by various multisyllabic ones (Monaghan and Barry 1999, 5). Orthography—the learning of the ABCs, decoding, and spelling—was the primary method until the middle of the nineteenth century, when a sight word approach was introduced with the idea that reading and understanding whole words was more natural than identifying letter sounds and blends (Pressley et al., 4). At this point, reading for meaning and comprehension became an additional, if not new focus of the instruction and methodology of the day. Progressive educators of the nineteenth century also introduced the concept of play as child's work and encouraged reading instruction from a child's own stories dictated to a teacher or written by the child's own hand (Monaghan and Barry 1999, 28).

Religious, cultural, and philosophical influences played a crucial role in the choice of reading instruction until the latter part of the twentieth century, when research through science began to analyze the efficacy and outcomes of one method over another. These divergent early American approaches, each with their theories for teaching literacy, parallel the "reading wars" controversy of the last fifty years. Looking a bit more closely at the development of reading instruction from the last half of the twentieth century brings to light how this significant facet of America's education revolved around a wheel of continual reinvention.

Dick and Jane—The Revolutionary Breakthrough

The first decades of the twentieth century brought about an emphasis on reading curriculums with a distinct focus on a child's point of view. During the 1920s and early 1930s, Dr. William S. Gray at Scott Foresman and Company conducted his own set of studies concluding that reading instruction for young children ought to reflect real-life situations with which young readers can identify. He theorized reading instruction also should be directed from detailed teacher guides to incorporate whole-word reading (titled the "look-say system") and include primers, workbooks, flash cards, and charts. Working with an editorial team led by reading consultant Zerna Sharp, a new set of textbooks featuring "attractive illustrations, large legible print, and well-written stories full of humor, action, climaxes, and suspense" were created centered around a new set of story characters (Kismaric and Heiferman 1996, 21). For the next four decades, children would come to know these characters as the idyllic Dick and Jane. The Foresman reading curriculum was an educational breakthrough not just because it attempted to reflect children's experiences and interests, but also because it took the concepts of whole-word recognition and the alphabetic principle previously used separately or together and created a series of graduated textbooks that addressed reading readiness through pre-primers and primers.

- Children were acquainted with reading through a contextual combination of pictures and short simple sentences.
- Teachers were given specific guidelines on incorporating phonics lessons within each story lesson.
- Controlled vocabulary was introduced using a limited number of new words in a repetitive pattern.
- Picture reading led to text reading.
- Comprehension was brought into the instruction as children learned to infer from what they were looking at and reading simultaneously.
- Textbooks became increasingly more difficult with new characters as they progressed to higher classes right through grade eight.

Gray also was cognizant of maintaining a certain moral element to reading instruction by including values lessons in the various stories and situations Dick, Jane, and subsequent characters encountered. As the 1960s approached, a variety of factors influenced how the Dick and Jane textbooks needed to change. But the program eventually fell out of favor with administrators, educators, parents, and politicians. Television-based children's programming, diversity, multiculturally oriented curriculums, and newly based scientific research among other factors helped to move reading instruction away from Gray's original concept. With a significant portion of the elementary school population experiencing difficulty in learning to read, new research and theories began to appear, spearheaded by Rudolf Flesch in his 1955 Harper & Row publication *Why Johnny Can't Read and What You Can Do About It*. Flesch was the first to criticize the Dick and Jane approach to reading instruction through a predominantly word recognition program and recommended phonics as the only effective method to teach reading (Chall 1967, 3).

The Alphabetic Principle—Phonics Leads the Way

Flesch's publication led the way to a range of new reading programs that primarily emphasized teaching the child to break the "reading code." Two approaches to (or theories about) teaching phonics were identified by educators, who now fell into two distinct camps. In her classic book *Learning to Read: The Great Debate*, Jeanne Chall used the term "intrinsic phonics" to describe analytic phonics-reading instruction that incorporates phonetic study of words already mastered through the sight word method. The other camp insisted on the "synthetic" teaching of letters, sounds, and their combination into blends before word recognition. They felt that their approach to the teaching of the reading code worked better, as children were able to sound out more difficult vocabulary and then move more readily into the comprehension stage of reading.

For the next twenty or so years, from the 1960s to the 1980s, a variety of programs were developed that either focused on the analytic or the synthetic phonetic method of initial reading instruction. Some programs were heavy with phonics rules, while others attempted to combine phonics with writing and spelling lessons. Still others used approaches that included "reading for meaning," with short stories printed in basal readers (Chall 1967, 24). There was even a linguistic approach developed by Leonard Bloomfield, who insisted that a child's verbal knowledge should be matched with the "teaching of the printed equivalents for his oral vocabulary" (Chall 1967, 24). This linguistic approach deemphasized comprehension and encouraged phonetic knowledge first. Bloomfield felt that meaning would naturally develop as the reading code was acquired. As Chall points out in her study, this difference of opinion concerning phonics over meaning presented a difference in the definition of beginning reading. Some favored a definition that placed word recognition ahead of meaning, appreciation, and use of the skill. Others promoted the meaningful interpretation of symbol reading as the ultimate goal. Should reading be taught with a vocabulary-controlled emphasis on meaning, or with an earlier start to the alphabetic principle prior to the simple stories? Chall's conclusions from her original studies published in her first edition (1967) were still supported as she claimed in her third edition update "The Evidence: Research on Beginning Reading Instruction,"

> *Although knowledge of letters and their sound values does not assure success in reading, it does appear to be a necessary condition for success. In fact, it seems to be more essential for success in the early stages of reading than high intelligence and good oral language ability. (Chall 1996, 84)*

As a result, the basal readers that were created and rewritten throughout the second half of the twentieth century until the early 1990s began to emphasize phonics and decoding at an earlier stage, combined with some of the previous meaning and comprehension strategies of the earlier readers.

Basal Readers—Did Reading Instruction Really Change?

Since the first publication of the Dick and Jane series, basal readers have become a huge focus and financial investment for the educational publishing world. Recognizing that the research findings, whatever they claimed to indicate, would impact sales, publishers began to incorporate and change the approach used in basal readers. Yet when evaluated closely, these series continued to "retain many of the pedagogical techniques in the old basals" (Pressley et al., 14). Phonics was either approached individually or embedded within the framework of each story lesson. Meaning was almost always taught through a series of questions after the passages. The important difference was the content of the stories, the diversity of the characters, the less rigid control of vocabulary, and the lengthy accompanying teacher's guides. Teachers were given more and more guidance as to how to work with each lesson with numerous follow-up activities that in some cases included an actual script to follow. In addition, educational publishers began to rely on children's literature, rewrite it, or mold it to fit certain reading levels designed within their basal program. But inevitably some children still struggled or failed to learn to read. Critics emerged once again with all sorts of reasons, the most popular summarized as follows:

- There were no universal generalizations for teaching phonics and the phonetic principles.
- The "good literature" when rewritten was creating stories that were vapid and dull.

- Basals required dividing children into reading groups, thereby creating an atmosphere of low self-esteem for the lowest achieving children (Porter 2006, 125).

In the 1950s, while educational publishers were busy developing basal reader programs amidst the reading instruction debates, two trade publishers, Harper & Brothers and Random House, came out with a new concept for beginning readers. At Harper, legendary editor Ursula Nordstrom received a manuscript that had been hand-delivered to her assistant, Susan Carr Hirschman, by a former first-grade teacher, Else Holmelund Minarik. Simultaneously, Nordstrom also received a request from friend, Boston public children's librarian Virginia Haviland, about the need to create stories for the child just breaking into the world of reading, the child who will triumphantly exclaim for the first time "I can read!" (Lodge 1997, 33; Silvey 2004, 54). With the supervision of the educationally cognizant Minarik, and the incredible illustrations of the young Maurice Sendak, Nordstrom created a very carefully designed new children's book for the novice reader. The literary quality of the innovative easy-reading format of *Little Bear* launched the successful I Can Read series.

In the early 1970s, as a new children's librarian in training at the Queens Public Library, I was privileged to attend a session led by Hirschman. Her passionate and sensible explanation behind the history and philosophy of the I Can Read series has stayed with me to this day. Hearing her personal version of how this concept began was most revealing on how reading should be encouraged and promoted. Hirschman recounted the careful consideration given to the layout of text intended to maintain spacing between lines with as much open "air" as possible. She told us how lines should be no more than forty characters long with sentences breaking at natural phrases so that children can read as they speak, naturally stopping at the end of a phrase in order to take a breath. This basic philosophy continues today with a wealth of titles both classic and newly added to the list each year. Nonfiction and fiction alike, I Can Read titles are published with editors and writers "relying on instinct rather than word lists or strict vocabulary rules, allowing the pictures to define the stories and help readers decode the words" (Lodge 1997, 33).

Challenged by a statement in a 1954 *Life* magazine article written by Pulitzer Prize-winnng author John Hersey, Ted Geisel worked for more than a year to create an alternative reading primer to the "boring Dick and Jane, omnipresent in American schools" (Lodge 2007). The result was *The Cat in the Hat* (1957), written in 236 words. With its new Beginner Books imprint created in 1958, Random House published *The Cat in the Hat Comes Back* (1958), the second in a highly successful, long line of patterned rhyming beginning reading books (Lodge 2007).

Simultaneously, as the criticism and controversy fueled the debate of best reading instruction practice, an entirely new focus was developing in the background that would soon emerge and take over for the latter part of the twentieth century.

Whole Language —Misused and Misunderstood

Striving to address the shortcomings of basal instruction, a philosophy now began to emerge and take hold focused on the need to integrate the basic skills of reading with the simultaneous application of the language arts of speaking, listening, reading, and writing. In a 1978 commentary essay in the journal *Language Arts*, editor Julie Jensen wrote about the "imbalance between too much attention to drill on the component skills of language and literacy and too little attention to their significant use" (Cazden 1992, 3). She continued with this statement that is at the core of the terminology "whole language":

> *Acquisition of such skills requires two things: first, practice of the component skills so that subroutines are run off automatically and attention can be focused at higher levels; and second, the availability of opportunities for the integration of the component parts into larger, meaningful wholes. (Cazden 1992, 3)*

New approaches were introduced that began to include basal readers with more predictable texts. Teacher-directed writing through children's own language, experience, activities, and responses to the stories read were now valued more than the drills and skills worksheets of the past. The much-criticized child-invented spelling was welcomed as opposed to the ritual memorization of weekly spelling lists. Over time, the intention was for children to transition to correct spelling through their reading and writing encounters. Perhaps the most important development of the whole language approach was the encouragement and introduction of trade children's literature in both the classroom library and reading curriculum. Children's publishing of trade books soared in the 1980s and 1990s as a result of the whole language infusion in the schools and reading curriculum (Pressley et al., 19).

But for numerous scholars, defining the purpose and methodology behind whole language became difficult. B. S. Bergeron (1990) identified six components:

- construction of meaning
- functional, relevant language
- literature
- writing process
- cooperative student work
- student effect (Jeynes and Littell 2000, 23)

Others, including Stahl and Miller (1989), reflected on the

- use of children's own language,
- child-centered as opposed to teacher-centered classrooms,
- large use of trade literature over basal readers, and
- intrinsic approach to the teaching of phonics as opposed to phonics taught in isolation (Jeynes and Littell 2000, 23).

If defining whole language proved difficult, implementing it successfully was an even greater issue. Teachers were given training or expectations that included direction for organizing and changing the classroom environment with, in some cases, minimal support (Walmsley and Adams 1993, 272). Teachers accustomed to prepackaged basal programs were now told to build a new literacy program from scratch using big books, independent reading time, reading and writing conference time, and project work in small group settings. Recommended attributes and features included:

- an abundance of trade literature throughout the curriculum
- lots of print around the room
- colorful, inviting classrooms that encouraged children moving around centers freely
- independent reading of child-selected books
- shared cooperative learning (Walmsley and Adams 1993, 278)

Lack of supportive and proper training created confusion and stress among teachers who found it difficult to simultaneously maintain and cover the traditional basics of phonics, spelling, grammar, and reading comprehension. The controversy began to develop not just with the general public and parents, who did not understand the concept, but within schools and among faculty who were divided between teachers who were involved in whole language practice and teachers who felt isolated and overwhelmed by the demands of this new child-centered classroom.

Nevertheless, whole language classrooms did in many situations produce positive outcomes, as noted in the study by Dahl and Freppon (1995). A cross-curricular comparison of first-grade classrooms in inner-city settings indicated there was little difference in the phonics knowledge gained, but rather a wide difference in how children applied their phonics knowledge to their reading. This represented a difference in a child's understanding of what literacy entailed in terms of a distinction between literacy skills and literate behaviors. The strategies applied to the whole language method allowed children to respond to literature in more sophisticated ways, as proficient readers do through reflection, writing, and discussion (p. 68).

Another effective teaching aspect of the whole language theory was the concept of working from a constructivist perspective. "The constructivist view of learning puts learners in the role of active participants. Teachers holding this view expect children to take on the role of active participant and be responsible readers" (Freppon and McIntyre 1999, 206). Russian educational psychologist Lev Vygotsky's zone of proximal development (ZPD) learning concept supports a theory of working within a student's ability and knowledge to bring about improvement and success through careful teacher scaffolding and monitoring. Teachers creating classrooms using cognitive models that allowed children to work within their ZPD were more likely to achieve reading knowledge, improvement, and success as the students were given greater learning responsibility.

By the late 1990s, two distinct views developed surrounding the two approaches and terminology of whole language and code emphasis instruction, each with its own misinterpretations or misperceptions that may still hold true today. The mere term "whole language" seems to invoke "an uninformed and irresponsible effort to finesse necessary instruction with 'touchy-feely' classroom gratification; while 'code emphasis' is translated into an unenlightened commitment to unending drill and practice at the expense of the motivation and higher-order dimensions of text that make reading worthwhile" (Adams 1998, 25–26). Unfortunately, the worthwhile principles of whole language that fostered huge improvement in attitudes about reading and overall reading skills were unintentionally forgotten with the idea that correctness in terms of "flawless final writing drafts" developed from quality children's literature-based reading programs did not matter, when in fact they did. Renowned literacy professor and children's author Mem Fox states:

> *Teachers forgot to tell children that writing is essentially a message from inside one head to inside other heads, and that when the message is ill-spelt, ill-organised, and expressed in an ill grammar, so to speak, the message gets badly mangled. (Fox 2001, 107)*

As the decade wore on, study after study emerged, offering a middle ground alternative to the phonics versus whole language debate. Two assessments, in particular, the book *Beginning to Read* by Marilyn Jager Adams (1990) and the final report *Preventing Reading Difficulties in Young Children*, written by a panel on the National Research Council (Snow, Burns, and Griffin 1998), coined a new philosophy and phrase, "balanced literacy."

Balanced Literacy—The Voice of Reason in a Wilderness of Controversial Debate

Much in the way Chall's (1996, 1967) "First Grade Studies" and comparisons of methodology concluded that a skills-based instruction was a necessary component to early reading success, Marilyn Jager Adams (1990) brought a renewed defense for knowledge of the alphabetic principle. Adams's observations of the previous research summarized three interpretations of phonics as required ingredients to beginning reading instruction.

• How much and what specific focus on phonics is enough to make a program effective?

• Which program is the best to accomplish the goal of reading instruction when each program proposes different assumptions and activities related to student needs?

• Which core number of phonics activities is most effective on a broad scale? (Adams 1998, 48–53)

Taking these three interpretations one step further, Adams posed the conclusion that sounding out words is *not* the primary outcome of phonics instruction when reading independence is the goal. Adams states:

> *Laboratory research indicates that the most critical factor beneath fluent word reading is the ability to recognize letters, spelling patterns, and whole words effortlessly, automatically, and visually. The central goal of all reading instruction—comprehension—depends critically on this ability. (Adams 1998, 54)*

Adams proposed the introduction of phonemic awareness (orally dividing speech sounds within words) as early in a child's life as possible, even earlier than the traditional first-grade initiation. She termed these children "prereaders," youngsters who were at a preschool age and not receiving formal reading instruction (Adams 1998, 55). She reasoned that children who were exposed to literacy in the home prior to formal schooling in the form of read-alouds, alphabet awareness, letter/sound correlation, phoneme (sound units) manipulation tasks, and nursery rhymes held an advantage over those who came to school without any type of literacy experience (pp. 80–81). Adams evaluated the processes of skillful readers. She looked at whether they:

- decipher word shape cues
- rely on some instinctive or sophisticated guessing
- use prediction or anticipation to formulate comprehension
- incorporate semantic clues
- sound out words when they cannot interpret whole words

She concluded that one or more strategies do not make a reader more skilled, but rather the use of *all* these methods together and in concert is what makes a skillful reader (Adams 1998, 95–105). Phonics is the one essential component to the reading activity *equal* to all the others. A balanced approach to instruction allows for all the components of reading instruction to work together "within a single integrated and interdependent system" (Adams 1998, 423).

Adams's conclusions and recommendations were well received, although with some caution as stated in the afterword by educators Dorothy Strickland and Bernice Cullinan. They asserted that the process of becoming literate is an ongoing development that cannot be categorized in three groups of non-readers, pre-readers, and readers (Strickland and Cullinan 1998, Adams, 427). The term "emergent readers" more correctly indicates that children are in a continued stage of literacy development with no particular starting point. Strickland and Cullinan also strongly emphasized the use of phonics within the context of reading and writing in a program that saturates children with good stories and opportunities to engage in literacy behaviors through intriguing play, performance, and their own writing experiences. This is the basis of a strong, balanced language arts curriculum.

The Committee on the Prevention of Reading Difficulties in Young Children provided some conclusive recommendations on how to "provide an integrated picture of how reading develops and how reading instruction should proceed" in order to prevent early reading failures (Snow, Burns, and Griffin 1998, vi). The recommendation coupled direct phonics instruction with a focus on reading for meaning and learning. Seeking to address the reasons for continued reading difficulties and failures in a portion of the early grade population, the committee outlined some key principles that sensibly apply to most children in first- through third-grade classrooms. Early reading instruction, they purported, must include:

- use of reading to obtain meaning from print
- frequent, intensive opportunities to read
- exposure to frequent, regular spelling-sound relationships
- learning about the nature of the alphabetic writing system
- an understanding of the structure of spoken words (Snow, Burns, and Griffin 1998, 3)

These principles are further employed by providing:

- a working understanding of how sounds are represented alphabetically
- sufficient practice to achieve fluency (automatic fluid reading) with a variety of texts
- sufficient prior knowledge and vocabulary to make written text meaningful and interesting
- metacognitive (self-corrective) strategies to monitor comprehension and misunderstandings
- constant motivation and interest to continue reading for a variety of purposes (Snow, Burns, and Griffin 1998, 3–4)

The committee acknowledged that an integrated approach would still miss the child who has difficulty understanding and using the alphabetic principle, transferring the comprehension skills of spoken language to reading, and feeling motivated to read. Because starting off right is the best way to address these issues, it was deemed imperative that teachers receive the correct training through professional development and optimal support to provide well-prepared, excellent instruction. Every primary-grade classroom should provide "the full array of early reading accomplishments: the alphabetic principle, reading sight words, reading words by mapping sounds to parts of words, achieving fluency, and comprehension" (Snow, Burns, and Griffin 1998, 6).

In many classrooms today, balanced literacy is practiced in a constructivist approach, even as new challenges are being directed at educators from politicians and policy makers. We have come a long way in terms of creating and re-creating effective reading instruction that borrows from the original Dick and Jane methodology grouped under a new umbrella of balanced literacy. Whether you call it word recognition or the look-say method, phonics or the alphabetic principle, phonemic awareness or emergent literacy, it all contributes to a child's reading instruction when applied together in a balanced approach.

Balanced literacy instruction in the late twentieth and early twenty-first centuries has succeeded in achieving greater results yet, in many instances, is still criticized for its inability in helping the struggling reader. Where we are today in this regard is where we have been, yet new approaches are continually implemented and in place to address this issue.

References

Adams, Marilyn Jager. *Beginning to Read: Thinking and Learning about Print*. Cambridge, MA: The MIT Press, 1990.

Cazden, Courtney B. *Whole Language Plus: Essays on Literacy in the United States and New Zealand*. New York: Teachers College Press, 1992.

Chall, Jeanne S. *Learning to Read: The Great Debate*. Fort Worth: Harcourt Brace College Publishers, 1996.

Chall, Jeanne S. *Learning to Read: The Great Debate*. New York: McGraw-Hill, 1967.

Dahl, K. L., and P. A. Freppon. "A Comparison of Inner-City Childrens' Interpretations of Reading and Writing Instruction in the Early Grades in Skills-Based and Whole-Language Classrooms." *Reading Research Quarterly* 30 (1995): 50–74. Retrieved January 16, 2007, from ERIC database.

Fox, Mem. "Have We Lost Our Way?" *Language Arts* 79, no. 2 (November 2001). Retrieved December 1, 2006, from http://www.memfox.net.

Freppon, Penny A., and Ellen McIntyre. "A Comparison of Young Children Learning to Read in Different Instructional Settings." *The Journal of Educational Research* 92 (4) (March/April 1999): 206–18.

Geisel, Ted. *The Cat in the Hat.* New York: Random House, 1957.

Geisel, Ted. *The Cat in the Hat Comes Back.* New York: Random House, 1958.

Jeynes, William H., and Stephen W. Littell. "A Meta-analysis of Studies Examining the Effect of Whole Language Instruction on the Literacy of Low-SES Students." *The Elementary School Journal* 101 (21) (September 2000). Retrieved September 1, 2006, from Professional Collection via Thomson Gale, http://find.galegroup.com.

Kismaric, C., and M. Heiferman. *Growing Up With Dick and Jane: Learning and Living the American Dream.* San Francisco: HarperCollins, 1996.

May, Frank. "The Sam Trap: A Primer in Applebet" in *Reading as Communication* (pp. 12–29). Columbus, OH: Charles E. Merrill Publishing, 1982.

Minarik, Else Holmelund. *Little Bear.* New York: Harper & Row, 1957.

Monaghan, E. Jennifer, and Arlene L. Barry. *Writing the Past: Teaching Reading in Colonial America and the United States, 1640–1940.* Newark, DE: International Reading Association, 1999.

Porter, Sara M. "Team Up With Teachers" in Phyllis Blaunstein and Reid Lyon (eds.) *Why Kids Can't Read: Challenging the Status Quo in Education* (pp. 121–136). Lanham, MD: Rowman & Littlefield Education, 2006.

Pressley, M., R. L. Allington, R. Wharton-McDonald et al. *Learning to Read: Lessons from Exemplary First-Grade Classrooms.* New York: Guilford, 2001.

Silvey, Anita. *100 Best Books for Children.* Boston: Houghton Mifflin, 2004.

Snow, Catherine E., M. Susan Burns, and Peg Griffin. *Preventing Reading Difficulties in Young Children.* Washington, DC: National Academy of Sciences—National Research Council, 1998. Retrieved January 4, 2007, from ERIC database.

Walmsley, Sean A., and Ellen L. Adams. "Realities of 'Whole Language': (Interview with Teachers Practicing the Whole Language Approach)." *Language Arts* 70 (April 1993): 272–279.

CHAPTER 2

Innovative Approaches for the Struggling Reader

A few years ago, when I entered the MAT in reading and language arts degree program, I worked closely with several struggling readers in the university's reading clinic. One, a first grader who came from a very dysfunctional home environment, could recognize only half of the letters in the alphabet. We worked together diligently creating a basic illustrated alphabet book that fostered letter recognition and sound correlation. What this boy really responded to were rhyming alphabet stories that I brought into the reading clinic, based on my years as a children's librarian and knowledge of good children's literature. This boy was bright enough to "get it," but had not been exposed enough to any of the pre-reading or emergent reading activities to put it all together. Another boy, a third grader, came to the clinic and read aloud fairly well. He read everything I gave him, yet when we began to talk about the story and the characters, he seemed lost and uninterested. Even though his reading of the words on the page was adequate, he struggled to comprehend. According to his parents, his reading level had scored at the second half of the first grade, almost two years below. However, when I read aloud to him, his listening was quite good, and we could then discuss the passage. I had to help this boy develop comprehension strategies that allowed him to keep his mind on the meaning of the passage and not just the words he was reciting individually and so confidently without any semblance of stringing them together for understanding.

Despite numerous studies and methods of instruction, classroom teachers and parents are still faced with some children who struggle to achieve reading success, often falling further behind while their peers strive ahead. These strugglers, however, cannot all be lumped into one category. A struggling reader may be a child who has difficulty grasping letter/sound correlations or one who reads a word list well but lacks proficiency in comprehending groups of words within sentences and paragraphs. Many struggling readers master the basics of phonics but have trouble building a list of words they can readily recognize without the need to sound them out.

Word recognition is crucial for developing mastery in reading, and certainly one of the factors in helping a struggler succeed. If you think about the way you read as an adult, your years of practice, if you will, have allowed you to acquire a long list of words you easily recognize. When you, as a more proficient reader, read a passage or page, you rarely need to sound out any words because you easily recognize most of them. If, however, you are reading something that is unfamiliar, such as a description of a medical procedure, many of the terms will seem foreign and you will revert to your phonics skills to sound out the unfamiliar words. Struggling readers who have not built enough of a word bank of sight words continually revert to sounding out each word, consequently concentrating on phonics rather than the groups of words on the page. Lack of enough word recognition slows down the reading process, preventing what reading specialists refer to as fluency—reading with a certain speed, accuracy, intonation, and phrasing (Allington 2006, 91). And without fluency, strugglers lose not only their confidence, but the comprehension that is the basis for meaningful reading. Reading becomes a chore, a difficult task, and a drudge that is unpleasant and uninviting.

Like phonics, fluency is only one component of successful reading. Simply reading words without the context of meaning prevents readers from achieving comprehension, the critical goal of reading. Education professor John J. Pikluski (1997) notes the importance of developing a definition of reading that

> *provides an important perspective for evaluating approaches to teaching word-identification skills. Most educators would agree that the major purpose of reading should be the construction of meaning—comprehending and actively responding to what is read.*

Both the International Reading Association and the National Council of Teachers of English consider reading to be "a complex, interactive process, using basic skills and advanced strategies to make meaning" (Braunger and Lewis 2006, 3). One of the clearest definitions of reading today is the one developed by the Michigan Department of Education, which states:

Reading is the process of constructing meaning through the dynamic interaction among the reader's existing knowledge, the information suggested by the written language, and the context of the reading situation.

The reader's interactive process involves using what he or she is already familiar with and knows (prior knowledge) with skills already acquired so that he or she can connect with the context of the written text. This process allows the reader to develop comprehension and make sense of what is written and what is read. Struggling readers tend to focus on letter/sound and word identification, leaving by the wayside the meaning they should be constructing from the printed text. Understanding how good readers approach reading and how their conscious and unconscious behaviors allow them to interact with text to construct meaning presents a way to develop new training for struggling readers.

Today, early elementary classrooms operating in a balanced literacy environment incorporate many of the traditional phonics concepts through rhyming activities, word family lists, word wall bulletin boards, and personal word banks to develop an abundance of word recognition. Fluency is strengthened through a variety of modeled repeated readings, self-monitoring techniques, and self-corrective strategies. These metacognitive principles are crucial in enabling struggling readers to rely on their own ability to decipher a difficult sentence or passage with a few simple strategies, rather than to stop and wait to be corrected by an adult, parent, or tutor every time they get stuck. Reducing the number of instances when adult intervention is necessary provides struggling readers with the extra confidence to continue to develop their reading more proficiently. So what are some of the strategies that work for good readers that can be stressed and encouraged with struggling readers?

Self-Corrective Strategies

For a struggling reader, getting stuck is one of the most frustrating aspects of reading. Many teachers today employ a series of "getting unstuck" tactics to help the struggler achieve success.

Simple books that utilize well-oriented pictures allow the reader to first look for clues within the illustration. Teaching the child to examine the word itself and to look for a chunk or part that she already recognizes is another step. Next, sounding out the word and then rereading may help. Likewise, encouraging the use of prior knowledge by connecting the unfamiliar word to a word already known may apply. Skipping the word or reading ahead and then going back to reread with a context sensible insertion for the unfamiliar word is another strategy. Finally, allowing the child to reread to see if the sentence applies and makes sense within the rest of the passage's context encourages meaning-making.

Providing opportunity through alternate shared reading aloud and rereading practice lets the struggler build on that crucial fluency to achieve normal pacing, accuracy, intonation, and phrasing with increased knowledge and insight of what he or she is reading. Language experience activities (LEA) encourage a child's creativity through the development of her own story that she either writes or is written down for her by an adult. Subsequent reading and rereading of the child's personal story becomes increasingly familiar and helps to build these necessary fluency skills as well (Cramer, 315).

Of course, frustrating a struggler further is not the point; providing help along the way when the strategies are not working is just as important as engaging struggling readers in their own abilities to work it out themselves by making sense of what they are reading.

If mastering fluency is one of the most important aspects of reading development, then comprehension follows. In their groundbreaking book about reading comprehension, *Mosaic of*

Getting Unstuck

Use pictures for clues.
Sound it out and go back and reread.
Does it make sense?
Look for chunks already known within the word.
Connect to a word already known.
Go back and reread.
Does it make sense?
Skip ahead, then reread.
What word fits in the sentence?
Does it make sense?

Thought (1997), Ellin Oliver Keene and Susan Zimmermann explore the various pieces of a mosaic created through a reader's cognitive thinking that must come together as a whole for reading with meaning to take place. Evaluating the various metacognitive skills proficient readers use as they read for understanding allows teachers to clearly grasp and model easily adaptive strategies to facilitate reading comprehension. These include

- thinking skills that activate a reader's prior knowledge about the topic or story,
- selecting or determining the important ideas in the text,
- creating mental questions about the text and what the author is saying,
- visualizing any images from the text,
- drawing conclusions and interpretations,
- summarizing or retelling, and
- using "fix-up" strategies when necessary to continue reading with comprehension (Keene and Zimmermann 1997, 22–23).

Think about your own engagement when you are reading something for the first time. You probably notice the title or heading first and make a prediction about what you think will take place or be said in the subsequent passage, article, or chapter. You might skim ahead a bit to get a quick idea, but more likely you will begin reading and, if you are consciously engaged, you will concentrate by thinking about what the author is intending. You may create an image in your mind of the scenario described, question or comment silently, use your prior knowledge to create inferences, and come away with a brief capsule or summary as you finish reading. Clearly you have unconsciously made sense of what you have read using these strategies.

Often, children who are just reading words, even if they are fluent, can complete a full paragraph or passage and not have any idea of the subject or the meaning of what they read. Mind-wandering as opposed to mind-monitoring is one of the challenges poor or unengaged readers face. Teachers tackle this by teaching comprehension strategies that employ prediction, visual mental images, prior knowledge, questioning and commenting, making connections with their own lives and other texts they have read, inferring meaning, and summarizing by determining themes and main ideas (Zimmermann and Hutchins 2003). In

Comprehension Techniques

Predict from title or headings.
Visualize the scenario.
Use prior knowledge.
Make connections to:

   Self
   Other texts
   Outside world

Infer other meanings.
Summarize ideas and themes.

(Modeled after Zimmermann and Hutchins 2003)

essence, they are teaching children to comprehend by having a mental conversation with the author as they are reading and self-monitoring their responses, just as you and other proficient readers do. Children who are reasonably good at reading a passage of words without creating a sense of understanding are taught to apply several comprehension techniques that good readers use.

All of these methods—phonics, fluency, word reading, and comprehension—are incorporated into a reading instruction curriculum that, if done correctly, allows children to learn from a teacher's use of the gradual release of responsibility model. What this means is that a teacher will follow an instructional plan that

- Demonstrates the actual strategy and provides a clear explanation of when and how to use it.
- Guides the student in the use of the demonstrated strategy.
- Allows the student to then independently apply the strategy learned and use it in self-monitored reading situations (Shanahan 2005, 31–32).

This simple model of *showing* a child how to work a strategy, *helping* the child work it out with you, and finally *releasing* the child to do it himself or herself is one of the basic tenets of today's teaching and learning approaches. When you think about it, most of us have learned a new skill, such as driving and cooking, with these three basic steps.

A variety of intervention programs for struggling readers have been in place for several decades, each with its own research and outcomes assessment for success. With the added focus on reading failure and improvement placed on schools and teachers following the implementation of No Child Left Behind, it is important for youth services librarians to be cognizant of the assortment and to understand the basic approaches, strategies, and goals for the programs prevalent in their school service area. While all intend to raise reading scores, the differences in methods and realization of improvement goals vary as well as the controversy in how funding is acquired, needed, or spent. Following is a summary of four programs that have been widely used and whose interventions and methods of instruction can and have been translated to regular classroom reading instruction.

Reading Recovery—Building from Individual Strengths

In the 1970s, New Zealand doctoral student Marie Clay researched and studied how all ranges of emergent readers were learning to read and write. She developed an understanding of how teaching reading should be designed close to the onset of instruction that would make a difference for the lower-achieving child (Schmitt 2005, 23). What became apparent from this was the concept that children, regardless of their difficulties in learning print, still display certain strengths and skills that can be used to build an individualized reading instruction program. This pioneering effort of working from individual strengths to address individual weaknesses grew to include a worldwide approach that incorporates support and training on three interlocking levels—university, school district, and local school building. Providing the slow learner an opportunity to receive individualized instruction within his own zone of proximal development is the crucial principle behind Reading Recovery. Marie Clay (1991) states:

> The teacher's task during that first year is to get the slow child responsive to instruction, happy to try and to discover for himself. . . . The essence of successful teaching is to know where the frontier of learning is for any one pupil on a particular task. (p. 65)

From this theory, the choice of reading materials would become as important as the individualized approach taken to achieve a graduated success in the struggling reader. Choosing texts written in a variety of styles to provide flexible strategies and approaches based on a child's own experiences proved to be a new way of creating a literacy learning library and introduced the leveled text concept in a collection of "little books."

In 1980, New Zealand author Joy Cowley created her Story Box series to provide some relevant reading materials in the New Zealand schools; she initiated a strong introduction to the concept of providing "little books" for reading instruction. Seeking to create suitable and easy texts for her son, who was having some reading difficulties, she began to write in the 1960s and became a pioneer in developing text that reflected a child's experiences. In an interview with the *New Zealand Listener* (1999), Cowley states:

> *A book should love and affirm a child in its content. Humour is vital. Children can't be tense about reading if they are laughing. The story should be exciting and I often put a twist at the end. . . . A book should be like a mirror which tells children how brave and beautiful they are. (http://www.wordpower.co.nz/cowley.html)*

The Story Box series, with its best-selling *Mrs. Wishy Washy*, proved highly successful with subsequent series and sales to educational distributors and publishers around the world.

What are the key points that make these "little books" so effective and successful for struggling readers that the traditional trade or basal readers miss?

- First is the flexibility of instruction through a short 100–200 word story, focusing on a child's experience and prior knowledge. The child can then move from one story to another as old learning is applied to new learning and as new challenges are presented through new stories at both the same and gradually increased levels.

- Second is the predictability of text, which helps a child anticipate how the text will continue from his or her own oral language, prior knowledge, repetitive sentence structure, or own knowledge of story structure. Predictability encourages a child to behave like a reader by using skills that he or she already has to understand spoken language and apply them to written text.

- Third is the extensive use of familiar texts that allows a child to further learn by rereading them numerous times. Like an actor practicing his or her lines, rereading familiar text will develop fluency, rhythm, and intonation, thus building confidence and independence.

Clay (1991) states this simply:

> *When children are allowed to reread familiar material they are being allowed to learn to be readers, to read in ways which draw on all their language resources and knowledge of the world, to put this very complex recall and sequencing behaviour into a fluent rendering of the text. (p. 184)*

In addition, the confidence and independence the child as reader develops helps him or her to rely on his or her own skills to support his or her reading rather than on the teacher's assistance. The text written for "little books" is carefully designed to reflect language that is natural rather than controlled, contrived, and stilted for phonetic emphasis or repetition. Contrived text that concentrates only on particular letter-sound relationships or particular genres presents more difficulties. We do not speak this way. Why should children read this way?

The struggling reader who has been exposed to contrived text is limited in the ability to relate what he or she already can do with language and apply it in books with new text. The original Dick and Jane series offers a contrived text designed by the number of times words are repeated using letter-sound relationships and the function of words in a sentence structure. Cowley's funny and much more realistic sequence of sentences in her story about a cow, a pig, and a duck experiencing the "lovely mud" allows the child to use language more naturally. A cow may jump into the mud, whereas a pig will naturally roll in it, and a duck might paddle (Cowley 1980). Equally important are illustrations—the key to matching text with action, enabling children to naturally know what to expect on each page. Controlled and contrived vocabulary prevents multiple inferences and meanings as well. Trade books have been better at this sort of simplified writing that is not contrived or stilted. The concept of a fur coat is subtly implied in "What Will Little Bear Wear" in Minarik's 1957 classic *Little Bear*. Little Bear removes his hat, coat, and snow pants to reveal his own fur coat. Multiple meanings in text allow children to bring what they know from their oral language experiences and gather new meaning with the text they are reading. Clay (1991) also asserts that contrived text for the sake of repetition is not necessary since high- and low-frequency words occur naturally without forced repetitions "because of the frequency principle in language" (p. 190). "Little books" are successful for struggling readers in that they provide another avenue of transition beyond the language experience approach. In addition to creating stories from the child's own oral knowledge and experience, the features of a printed story written in text within the natural oral language of children give the teacher flexibility in accommodating a child's individual needs.

In Reading Recovery, children are tutored individually in a pull-out program if they score below the twentieth percentile in their grade. Specially trained teacher/tutors employ a combination of LEA and "little books" to work as a flexible transition between oral language and literary text. Clay's theory and practical approach to developing an individualized reading program for struggling readers offers some basic steps to achieving confident, successful new readers. Children are taught problem-solving skills to uncover the meaning of text based on semantic, syntactic, and phonics cues. They are taught to interpret their own understanding of the reading process based on their own prior literacy and oral language. And they learn to monitor their own reading, check on themselves, and use their oral language as a resource while learning the regularities and exceptions of print.

> *The centerpiece of Reading Recovery is the development of readers who are self-regulated strategy users who move through text on their own, use word attack strategies on their own, monitor their own reading and comprehension, and use writing strategies (from the finger-spacing strategy to rereading their own text to see if it makes sense). (Pressley and Roehrig 2005, 13)*

But the Reading Recovery program also has its weaknesses and critics. For one thing, it targets a very small percentage of the struggling reader population, making individualized instruction extremely expensive. Estimates indicate the average Reading Recovery tutor helps only seven students per year with initial costs falling between $2,500 and $10,000 per student (American Federation of Teachers 1999, 21). In addition, because its principles stem from using context cues rather than decoding, the program has been criticized for its lack of explicit instruction in phonemic awareness and phonics as aligned with recent reading research studies. However, the extensive training Reading Recovery teachers must acquire can lead to translating many of the teaching concepts to general reading instruction within a regular first- to third-grade classroom.

Early Steps—Balanced and Comprehensive

Like Reading Recovery, Early Steps concentrates on serving the needs of first graders through specially trained teachers and Title

I tutors. Its main goal is reaching and correcting problems before readers reach the post-primary grades, where they will inevitably experience real reading failures (AFT 1999, 8). And much like its counterpart, comprehensive individualized instruction is created with a balanced approach that blends phonemic awareness and phonics instruction with word-study activities, writing, and language experience activities, rereading of familiar texts for fluency proficiency, and careful introduction of new reading at a graduated or slightly more difficult level. Costs serving a population of up to thirty children fall between $15,000 and $25,000 per student, taking into account the intensive professional development required for each teacher/tutor training. The combination of literature-based instruction to build on prior knowledge with comprehension and vocabulary skills for one-on-one teaching seems to show a high success rate for the bottom tier of at-risk first graders (AFT 1999, 9).

Direct Instruction—A Scripted Sequential Program

Highly structured with research-tested teaching scripts, Direct Instruction strives to accelerate learning for at-risk students across the elementary grades. The basic overall goal of the program is to move students to "mastery" as quickly as possible through a regimented series of fast-paced, scripted lessons followed by rhythmic choral reading and individual responses (AFT 1999, 4). Unlike the balanced approaches of Reading Recovery and Early Steps, skills here are taught in a sequence from phonemic awareness to complex phonics to decoding to comprehension to analysis, moving from one to the other only after full mastery is achieved. A rapid pace of teaching is noted for quick transition between skills together with grouping of students and frequent assessments. Use of coaches and facilitators for teacher training and mentoring is also applied during classroom time to reduce the extra costs of staff development. However, while it serves a wider population, a major criticism of this program is the structure and parroting of lessons that often stifle creativity and critical-thinking abilities to help struggling readers move themselves into more proficient, self-monitored reading positions. Nevertheless, teachers and mentors together have been able to successfully work within the framework of the structured lessons "to innovate within the repetition, so that [students and teachers] become drawn in as well" (AFT 1999, 6).

Exemplary Center for Reading Instruction (ECRI)— Strengthening and Supplementing Existing Curricula

Developed in the 1960s and 1970s, this program works within the framework of existing reading and language arts instruction already in place for all grades. Its instructional approach includes strategies for developing word recognition and vocabulary, study skills, spelling, literature, penmanship, literal, critical and interpretive comprehension, and writing (AFT 1999, 12). The teaching method includes three combined principles of modeling new concepts with at least seven different skills, prompting students to check for understanding to attain rapid, accurate responses and allowing students to practice independently as teachers hold individual conferences for re-teaching, testing, and small group discussions. Students are given the added expectation of responsibility requiring active participation in their own learning by providing them with skills to diagnose and correct their own errors (AFT 1999, 12). Like Direct Instruction, ECRI makes use of scripted lessons, with the idea of achieving mastery as quickly as possible. However, proper training of the use of these lessons with specific instructional techniques is what makes this program successful for struggling readers across the curriculum.

The above four programs are just a small example of the variety of research-based initiatives to provide successful interventions for struggling readers in many of today's schools. The interventions and specific instructional strategies involve either one-on-one targeted learning or structured sequential lessons. All involve detailed professional development as a base for successful implementation, focusing on basic concepts of phonemic awareness, phonics and decoding, word study and recognition, fluency, comprehension, and writing.

Every child entering school for the first time brings along his or her own personal advantages and disadvantages in what will either propel him or her forward or hold him or her back in achieving reading success. Evaluating all new readers, determining curricula, selecting methods of instruction, providing choice of materials, and complying with federal legislation that mandates adequate yearly school improvement can be a daunting and uneven task in a nationally fragmented educational system that depends on varying levels of funding and professional support.

To complete the picture of how achieving reading instructional success is difficult, and how librarians may play a more effective supporting role, we must factor in today's climate of research-based educational practices that conflict with political and educational publishing agendas.

References

Allington, Richard. *What Really Matters for Struggling Readers: Designing Research-Based Programs.* Boston: Pearson Education Inc., 2006.

American Federation of Teachers. *Building on the Best: Learning from What Works, Five Promising Remedial Reading Intervention Programs.* Washington, DC: American Federation of Teachers, 1999.

Braunger, Jane, and Jan Patricia Lewis. *Building a Knowledge Base in Reading.* Newark, Delaware: International Reading Association and Urbana, Illinois: National Council of Teachers of English, 2006.

Clay, Marie. *Becoming Literate: The Construction of Inner Control.* Portsmouth, NH: Heinemann, 1991.

Cowley, Joy. *Mrs. Wishy Washy.* DeSoto, TX: Wright Group/McGraw-Hill, 1980.

"Joy Cowley, Grand Dame of Children's Literature." *New Zealand Listener* (1999). Retrieved February 1, 2007, from http://www.wordpower.co.nz/cowley.html.

Keene, Ellin Oliver, and Susan Zimmermann. *Mosaic of Thought: Teaching Comprehension in a Reader's Workshop.* Portsmouth, NH: Heinemann, 1997.

Pikluski, John J. "Teaching Word-Identification Skills and Strategies: A Balanced Approach." Houghton Mifflin, 1997. Retrieved October 18, 2008, from http://www.eduplace.com/rdg/res/teach/def.html.

Pressley, Michael, and Alysia Roehrig. "Reading Recovery as Professional Development: Looking at Classroom Teachers." *Journal of Reading Recovery, Twentieth Anniversary Issue* (2005): 12–15.

Schmitt, Maribeth. "Changing the Educational Landscape: A Short History of Reading Recovery in North America." *The Journal of Reading Recovery, Twentieth Anniversary Issue* (2005): 22–30.

Shanahan, Timothy. *National Reading Report: Practical Advice for Teachers.* Naperville, IL: Learning Point Associates, 2005.

Zimmermann, Susan, and Chryse Hutchins. *7 Keys to Comprehension: How to Help Your Kids Read It and Get It!* New York: Three Rivers Press, 2003.

CHAPTER 3

What It All Means Today

Leveling—A Gradient of Difficulty

Twenty years ago, I was invited to a parent-teacher workshop at the local elementary school in my public library jurisdiction. At the height of the whole language reading instruction trend, I prepared a lengthy book talk, from picture books to easy readers, to early fiction and nonfiction, for an audience of parents and teachers eager to immerse their students in good children's literature. My knowledge at that time was minimal in terms of how my suggestions would really blend in with their reading strategies, but I was confident in my choices for quality trade books. The concept of how parents should read with their children to stimulate reading interest was the only one I addressed.

Fast-forward to 2007, when I attended a parent-teacher workshop targeted at kindergarten and first-grade families at a school where I volunteered in the literacy library. The purpose of this meeting was quite different, as the reading specialist explained specific strategies parents might use to help their children move ahead in independent reading. The book talk was also different, as the public librarian and the reading specialist blended their talks to include both the little leveled books that comprised the school's literacy library and how certain traditional trade easy readers could be used to work with children's reading instruction within the leveled concept.

Reading instruction in the new millennium reflects practices suggested by many of the educational research studies of the latter part of the twentieth century. A significant outcome of the balanced literacy approach has been the development of classroom literacy libraries filled with "little books," basal readers, and trade literature. These libraries are organized by levels that reflect gradients of difficulty.

Leveling involves a progression of small steps that move from very easy text to more complex reading situations. Rather than the readability formulas of the past, such as the Fry readability graph that factors the number of syllables for each 100 words, levels are determined by a variety of criteria that may include a text's repetitiveness, predictability, rhythmic language, and correlation of words and pictures—all concepts addressed by Marie Clay. Other progressions might include decodability through letter/sound relationships. These small steps accumulate in a wide range of difficulty within a specific grade level and enable teachers to individually select appropriate text for both independent reading and practice and group instruction. So, for example, in a second-grade classroom, the literacy library may include reading levels for grades 1–3 that are subdivided into small increments (1.1, 1.2, 2.1, 2.2, 3.1, 3.2, etc.). Arriving at these small increments can differ from program to program or classroom to classroom depending on the criteria used.

Sound confusing? It is, because in today's educational publishing empire, combining criteria for "little books," basal readers, and trade literature can vary greatly in terms of precise increments. Levels are not standardized from one publisher to another. More recently, two highly recognized experts in the field of literacy education, Irene C. Fountas and Gay Su Pinnell (2006), have developed an approach to assist teachers in leveling classroom libraries that incorporate both trade and "little books" simultaneously. They caution that teachers work together to establish specific benchmarks to follow when leveling a particular set or collection of books. Their suggested criteria take into account:

- genre and format
- structure or text organization
- content
- themes and ideas
- language and literary features
- sentence complexity
- vocabulary

- words to decode
- illustration support
- print features such as layout (p. 18)

Creating a gradient of difficulty is all well and good, but it is not an exact science. "Difficulty" is a vague term when children's abilities are concerned. What may prove to be easy for one child may be hard for another. Indeed, Clay asserts, "Gradients of difficulty are essential for teachers making good decisions about materials they select for children to read but all gradients are inevitably fallible" (1991, 201). Yet with all good intentions, publishers and schools have boarded the leveling and "little books" bandwagon to include thousands of "little books" in series, each with their own set and list of gradient levels. This has created a new process of matching and contrasting leveling charts that could make any teacher dizzy, let alone a school or public librarian.

Nevertheless, many teachers have grown to rely on leveling compatibility charts to code materials in their libraries with some semblance of accuracy. The point of all this is to create a reading environment in which children can have access to material they can read comfortably at their independent level and also be able to achieve learning with material that is available at their individual instructional level. These objectives behind leveling may result in both positive and negative outcomes in reading instruction.

The Leveling Craze

Seeking to provide appropriate support and learning within a range of abilities, many teachers today organize their classroom libraries to reflect levels of difficulty rather than genre, content, and format. This is happening with not just educational publications, but with the trade books that are in use from the whole language classroom environment. The problem with this approach is that a lot of time and energy is being devoted to reading levels that can ultimately prevent exposure to a wider range of learning. This "leveling mania," as termed by Karen Szymusiak and Franki Sibberson (2001, 16), can actually limit a child's access to the variety of book selection opportunities that speaks to the child's interests. A certain amount of variety is necessary to provide rich and diverse reading experiences that lead to greater independence as readers are exposed to increased pleasure in their readings (Dzaldov and Peterson 2005). As children become more independent, and hopefully continue to enjoy their reading experiences, they move from the basic learning phase into a transitional phase. Boxing children within a strictly leveled literacy library could likely prevent the smooth shift into the next phase of reading instruction for children in grades two and up. These transitional readers are defined as those possessing many strengths and a variety of weaknesses who readily and competently use decoding skills but need a different level of support strategies to sustain their reading comprehension and improvement (Szymusiak and Sibberson 2001). The transitional reader has specific needs and characteristics. She or he is learning about reading in these ways:

- to select appropriate books based not only on her level, but by personal needs and interests
- to sustain comprehension for longer texts
- to maintain interest over an entire book, short novel or nonfiction text
- to understand different genres and be able to make sense of any kind of text
- to maintain fluency with more difficult text which in turn maintains comprehension
- to use a variety of text features including nonfiction formats and fiction literary techniques—flashbacks, multiple characters, time, place, and settings (Szymusiak and Sibberson 2001, 9)

Good teachers understand not only the specific weaknesses that children have in the mechanics of learning to read, but are aware of how to foster and nurture the initial enthusiasm of reading by matching pupils with books based on their interests, motivations, sociocultural identities, and background experiences. Moving children along the levels ladder offers opportunities to scaffold instruction appropriately and also teaches students that the purpose of reading is to achieve at higher and higher levels. On the other hand, a classroom philosophy that offers selections from both a leveled collection and a school library organizational setting with ordering by author, genres, topics, etc., provides a wealth of choices and encourages children to use leveling as one aspect or tool among several when making their reading selections.

Moving Through the Leveling Ladder

Assessing individual abilities and reading levels has become the norm and is implemented through formal standardized testing. While these tests are widely used to determine and evaluate school and student achievement and performance, it is the informal tests that teachers employ with their individual pupils on a weekly or monthly basis that establishes the path of reading a child can follow in his or her schooling. The most common of these informal assessments is known as an informal reading inventory, or IRI.

Working with children in a leveled classroom library to allow independent and instructional reading has a specific intention based on the informal reading inventories teachers perform throughout the year. IRIs are administered in an informal way as children perform various reading and listening tasks during guided and individual reading lessons. The idea that children learn best when given the right level of reading material challenges teachers, parents, and librarians to find reading material that is just right for each reader to work with, master, and show progress. Four learning levels are established regardless of what grade the child is in when evaluating someone with an IRI.

Note their characteristics below:

Reading Levels and Their Characteristics

Independent level: This is the level of supplementary and recreational reading.

- Student is able to read fluently without assistance.
- Student is able to read independently with excellent comprehension.

   Instructional level: Here the student is challenged and remains interested, but is not frustrated.

- Oral reading may be less fluent, but retains some sense of rhythm and expression.
- Reads well enough to attain word recognition and comprehension with some instruction.

   Frustration level: The student is unable to read the material with adequate word recognition or comprehension.

- Numerous behavioral characteristics such as word-by-word reading and finger-pointing may be observed if students are attempting to read materials that are too difficult for them.

- Oral reading may exhibit lack of expression, and silent reading may include lip movement.
- Instruction is ineffective and progress is nil or minimal.

  Listening level: This is the highest level at which a student can understand material that is read *to* him

- This is an indication of reading potential when a substantial difference exists between a student's instructional level and listening level.
- It indicates a reader who should be able to make significant progress in reading achievement with appropriate teacher guidance.

Determining these levels through an IRI assessment is primarily done by a teacher or a tutor. Understanding the distinction between these levels is important when helping children with their reading selections. Remember that the results of the tests indicated below are an estimate of the reader's abilities. The percentages are a clear indication of why each level's characteristics are significant.

For a child to read with comfort and adequate comprehension, he or she must fall between a 90–100 percent range of no errors or competent self-correction instances. For the child to gain reasonable instruction, comprehension must fall between a 70–89 percent range of errors where corrective strategies are then encouraged and used. Anything less than 70 percent indicates a level where the child is frustrated and cannot improve because of a low level of comprehension. Children must have some prior knowledge or basis of comprehension upon which learning can take place and grow.

Informal reading inventories are administered for the purpose of finding general strengths and weaknesses in a child's reading and to diagnose any problematic patterns. Examples of this might include having no difficulty with recognizing words in a list, as

	Reading comprehension	Listening comprehension	Word recognition (in isolation)	Word recognition (in context)
Independent	90–100%	90–100%	90–100%	97–100%
Instructional	70–89%	70–89%	70–89%	90–96%
Frustration	69% or less	69% or less	69% or less	89% or less

Figure 3-1 Informal Reading Inventory (IRI) Assessment Table.

opposed to misreading, skipping, or substituting words in a con-textual situation that then changes the meaning of the piece. Does the child realize his or her error and self-correct most of the time? Does the child depend on help or use the various strategies will-ingly when stuck?

Ultimately, informal assessment, when done regularly and cor-rectly, serves as a model for observation of a child's reading in a more realistic setting to determine more of what he or she knows before addressing the child's needs. Building on these strengths is a positive method of instruction that has carried over from the last century's balanced literacy and early intervention programs for struggling readers.

The Politics of Reading Instruction

Federal legislation, first introduced in the 1960s with the Ele-mentary and Secondary Act of 1966 and its major funding com-ponent of Title 1, has in the last twenty years proceeded with the Comprehensive School Reform and Development Act of 1990 and the Reading Excellence Act of 1998. The No Child Left Behind Act of 2001 (NCLB) reauthorized the Elementary and Secondary Education Act of 1966 (ESEA), the main federal law affecting education from kindergarten through high school.

The much talked about government initiative connected with NCLB, Reading First, is a component much like Title 1, the fund-ing for remedial reading services. The difference is that Reading First is a "$1 billion-per-year initiative to help *all* children read at or above grade level by the end of third grade" and provides grants for programming that is deemed effective through scien-tifically based reading research (Gamse et al. 2008, 2). Reading First funding can be used for:

- *Reading curricula and materials* that focus on the five essential components of reading instruction as defined in the Reading First legislation: (1) phonemic awareness, (2) phonics, (3) vocab-ulary, (4) fluency, and (5) comprehension;
- *Professional development and coaching* for teachers on how to use scientifically based reading practices and how to work with struggling readers;
- *Diagnosis and prevention* of early reading difficulties through stu-dent screening, interventions for struggling readers, and moni-toring of student progress (Gamse et al. 2008, 2).

The basics as outlined above appear to be in tune with current reading instruction practices, yet the controversy and effectiveness have been questioned and critiqued for reasons that include unfairness, inflexibility, and inadequate funding.

NCLB aims to provide influence and accountability on local school districts and states for reading improvement. Congress established a concept of "adequate yearly progress" or AYP in order to close the achievement gap between low performing and high performing schools and students. Under NCLB, each state has developed and implemented measurements for determining whether its schools and local educational agencies (LEAs) are making adequate yearly progress.

AYP is an individual state's measure of progress toward the goal of 100 percent of students achieving to state academic standards in at least reading/language arts and math. It sets the minimum level of proficiency that the state, its school districts, and schools must achieve each year on annual tests and related academic indicators. (Ed. gov)

This latest bipartisan legislation (2004) requires states to create their own definitions of AYP to highlight where improvement is needed and where existing resources should be directed. Accountability is the key, with intended goals for measurable improvement for *all* students, therefore "leaving no child behind." And, of course, this measurable improvement is to be determined through standardized testing.

But, as reading specialist Richard Allington (2006) states, the former testing under Title 1 usually tested only struggling readers with "a demonstration of achievement growth roughly comparable to one year's gain" (p. 16). Under NCLB, all children in grades three to eight are tested with the goal of closing the achievement gap between strugglers and readers at grade level. If most strugglers are reading two to three years behind, closing the gap might mean that struggling readers must show more than one year's growth, which in most cases would be more growth than a grade-level reader would show in one year (Allington 2006, 17). And while states have been allowed to set their own standards for AYP, the overall goal of having all children read at a targeted level by 2014 has had its unintended and unfair consequences.

If a school fails to meet AYP within a two-year period, mandated corrective actions are put into place, often with additional financial impacts falling on the local district. The argument has been that pressure to meet these goals has either caused a lowering of standards by some states or a focus away from balanced literacy instruction with an emphasis on teaching to meet test requirements. This high-stakes testing focus removes much of a teacher's flexibility in applying methods to achieve goals of helping children understand reading strategies while they become literacy proficient, confident, and increasingly eager to read.

At the time of this publication, NCLB is in a holding pattern waiting for the new Congress in 2009 to reauthorize, change, or replace it. Some of the criticism has been considered, and it remains to be seen as to how the law's basic tenets and requirements might be altered. For now, it is important to understand that politicians today, as in the past, have tried to influence education for the better; yet it is educators and parents who play the crucial role.

NCLB's goals of providing instruction through the five basic methods of phonemic awareness, phonics, vocabulary, fluency, and comprehension are essential for any program and must be maintained in all early grade classrooms. Similarly, adequate professional support through staff reading coaches and staff development, as well as early intervention strategies in kindergarten and first grade with help provided by good, intensive instruction ensures catching slow or struggling children before they get lost and frustrated. Incorporating other measures of assessment with standardized testing should be another goal, so that a balanced education with a focus on the arts, sciences, and history play equal roles in a reading and math curriculum.

Children's and youth services librarians serving their communities can be more effective when armed with the knowledge of how reading instruction has evolved, changed, and is currently applied. Let's look at some ways to provide this service in our daily responsibilities, from readers' advisory to community involvement, school support, and collection development.

References

Adequate Yearly Progress, http://www.ed.gov/nclb/accountability/ayp/edpicks.jhtml.

Armbruster, Bonnie B., Fran Lehr, and Jean Osborn. *Put Reading First: The Research Building Blocks of Reading Instruction Kindergarten Through Grade 3, Second Edition.* Washington, DC: Center for the Improvement of Early Reading Achievement (CIERA), 2003.

Clay, Marie. *Becoming Literate: The Construction of Inner Control.* Portsmouth, NH: Heinemann, 1991.

Cox, Beverly E., and Carol J. Hopkins. "Building on Theoretical Princi-ples Gleaned from Reading Recovery to Inform Classroom Practice." *Reading Research Quarterly* 41 (2) (April/May/June 2006): 254–267.

Dzaldov, Brenda Stein, and Shelley Peterson. "Book Leveling and Read-ers." *The Reading Teacher* 59 (3) (November 2005): 222–229.

Fountas, Irene C., and Gay Su Pinnell. *Leveled Books (K–8): Matching Texts to Readers for Effective Teaching*. Portsmouth, NH: Heinemann, 2006.

Fry, Edward. *Elementary Reading Instruction*. New York: McGraw-Hill, 1977.

Gamse, B. C., H. S. Bloom, J. J. Kemple, and R. T. Jacob. *Reading First Impact Study: Interim Report* (NCEE 2008-4016). Washington, DC: National Center for Education Evaluation and Regional Assistance, Institute of Education Sciences, U.S. Department of Education, 2008.

"Key Policy Letters Signed by the Education Secretary or Deputy Secre-tary." July 24, 2002. Retrieved January 21, 2007, from http://www.ed.gov/print/policy/elsec/guid/secletter/020724.html.

Szymusiak, Karen, and Franki Sibberson. *Beyond Leveled Books: Support-ing Transitional Readers in Grades 2–5*. Portland, ME: Stenhouse Pub-lishers, 2001.

PART 2

The Reading Riddle and the Role of the Children's Librarian—Dovetailing Roles with Reading Instruction

The well-versed children's librarian plays different roles within the library and throughout the community. By providing reading instructional support within the context of these roles, you can significantly enhance your library's children's services. With this in mind, let's explore some of these roles.

CHAPTER 4

The Reading Advocate

The term "advocate" generally brings numerous thoughts to mind. Perhaps you are an advocate for your family, promoting healthy meals, providing advice, or encouraging your children's aspirations for their career goals. You may also be an advocate for your school district, supporting certain school board candidates at election time, assisting staff and children as a volunteer, or working closely on the PTO board. Or if you are an advocate for the environment, you favor recycling whenever possible, purchase energy efficient appliances, and so on. To advocate for a person, purpose, idea, or cause means to support, advise, encourage, favor, promote, endorse, and even campaign for or champion it. As a children's librarian, you play the role of advocate for your community, constituents, colleagues, and staff by providing support, advice, and encouragement for their needs, goals, and development.

However, your role as a children's librarian is, first and foremost, to be a reading advocate who supports literacy by:

- advising young readers
- stimulating emerging, new, and transitional readers
- encouraging struggling readers
- enticing proficient yet complacent readers
- cheering on avid, eager readers
- favoring good books and multimedia

- campaigning for intellectual freedom
- promoting literature-based programming
- endorsing lifelong reading for pleasure and information

A good reading advocate displays an empathy and clear understanding of the needs and abilities of the child reader. Determining these needs and abilities requires the psychological know-how and artistic skill of relating and interacting with the youngster (often along with a parent or caregiver) while simultaneously creating opportunities for that child to engage in meaningful reading and successful and pleasurable literacy experiences.

Advocating as a Reader's Advisor

A good children's library service maintains a balance between readers' advisory and reference or bibliographic guidance. Each situation encompasses, on your part as the librarian, a discerning interpretation of the child's simple request for a book and/or enthusiastic or timid inquiry. A youngster's articulation and ability to express needs and preferences can be as varied as the range of ages that come through the door.

In a 2001 *Public Libraries* article, Kay Bishop and Anthony Salveggi applied Piaget's theory of child development to the delivery of children's reference service. Reviewing some of the basics of Piaget's theory in light of children's services provides some psychological insight to the behaviors demonstrated in a child-oriented reference and advisory interview.

Very young children within the age span of two to seven are still quite egocentric and verbalize their requests as they understand them, unaware that their spoken interpretation may not be intelligible to the intended listening adult (Bishop and Salveggi 2001, 355). They may be eager and interrupt you when you're in the middle of another request from someone else. Because categories and subcategories are concepts they have yet to grasp, their questions may be verbalized as a broad theme and not truly indicate what their specific need may be (Bishop and Salveggi 2001, 355). For example, a young child may tell you she likes to read about animals, when in reality she is interested in cats and even more specifically newly born kittens.

According to Piaget's theory, older children ranging from ages seven to eleven more ably apply logical thought to concrete reasoning. They understand the concept of categorizing and can better and more specifically verbalize their likes, dislikes, and requests (Bishop and Salveggi 2001, 355). However, children in this older age range like to feel successful and self-confident in their ability to satisfy their interests. It is important to engage in a conversation with them that reiterates their comments for clarity while you walk them through the process of library exploration.

In today's overprotective world, it is less common that young-sters come to the library by themselves. Often, the children's li-brarian is approached by the child along with a parent, caregiver, or familiar adult. Children's librarians know that this "three-party transaction" (Bishop and Salveggi 2001, 357) offers more chal-lenges to accomplishing a successful interview for both child and librarian. Children's emotional readiness, intellectual ability, and social adeptness are continually evolving. The aid of an adult dur-ing a reference exchange may either speed up the child's interac-tion with the librarian with a very direct and quick, to-the-point inquiry, or may hamper it by creating some confusion with a mis-perceived assumption on the part of the adult. Cognizant of the differences between child and adult-child interactions, children's librarians become masters at simultaneously holding an interview with the child and adult by diplomatically moving, with finesse and great patience, from a child-oriented conversation to a reas-suringly respectful adult dialogue. Children's librarians know to apply etiquette and approachable body language with smiles, friendly nods, visual contact (particularly at the child's eye level), good humor, and instructive modeling of searching techniques.

Most importantly, in taking the time to understand their client group, children's librarians know to evaluate the cultural commu-nity they serve to better forge communication with their young patrons. In our diverse, and often immigrant communities, verbal and nonverbal communication often reflects specific customs. For example, Latino children may appear shy in making eye contact with the librarian; but in their culture, their restraint is really a mark of respect for an elder or authority figure.

Dovetailing Readers' Advisory and Reference with Reading Instruction

Library science educator and children's services expert Virginia A. Walter asserts that "readers' advisory for kids is an art because in addition to knowledge of the books and a knowledge of the child, it requires a kind of instinctive and creative ability to put the two together" (Salvadore 2001, 43). For a youth librarian, recommending books and informational reading choices that are appropriate for young patrons in terms of readability, interest, and, more importantly, their individual reading capabilities is more nebulous than concrete.

Teachers and parents have a more established presence in a child's reading life, with a clearer view on what will work for a particular youngster. Through a reference interview, librarians use their interpersonal skills to establish trust so that their conversational exchanges reveal clues as to where the child may be independently comfortable in terms of reading skills and what he or she will ultimately be willing to read with reasonable comprehension success. Gaining a sense of this can be more directly achieved by asking the parent if the child has been evaluated and where his or her range of independent and instructional levels falls. Distinguishing between the child's independent and instructional reading ability can make the difference in sending the child home with the prospect that he or she will return with a sense of satisfaction and accomplishment. And having an awareness of what is being offered in the classroom library can be crucial in providing suggestions from the public or school library's collection that complement the classroom's reading instructional goals. Chapter 7, "Keeper of the Tools," expands on key ways to maintain knowledge of both collections and to provide access through availability, compatibility, and portability.

Let's explore some of the reading instructional philosophy as it relates to each category of reader—emerging, new, transitional, struggling, and more proficient—through existing classic and newly published gems in children's trade literature prevalent in today's public and school library collections.

Emerging and New Readers

In early grade classrooms (K–2), reading instruction is often delivered through two approaches, shared reading and guided reading. In shared reading, the teacher displays a large poem or uses a big book to have children read along with him or her. The poem/story is read numerous times throughout the week so that these budding readers can visually and mentally begin to connect the letter/sound and word combinations with the printed squiggles or words on each page. This is usually done as a whole class activity and is the basis for several spin-off activities during the week.

Guided reading works a little differently; it is arranged by groups and organized to teach a specific skill and to encourage more independent reading and synthesizing. Classrooms may also include time for independent reading and partner reading, where children either read on their own or share a book with a fellow classmate (Hart-Hewins and Wells 1999, 44). Selections for these reading lessons reflect some of the components that are quite effective in the philosophy of the "little books" that provide emerging readers and new readers with:

- stories they can relate to based on their prior experience
- predictable situations they can anticipate
- repetitive but uncontrived language they can learn
- rhyming that also makes contextual sense
- picture cues that compliment and enhance narration

More and more picture books today reflect imaginative situations with intriguing language and artistic appeal, which make for good first reading choices. Emerging and new readers can benefit widely from such picture books that offer the above checklist, but are also categorized by a variety of predictable situations.

The circular story revolves around an interlinking action or activity that recurs throughout the plot and eventually returns to the beginning concept. These circular or cyclical stories may be extremely brief or may be more extensive and offer opportunities for much repetitive language. *If You Give a Mouse a Cookie* by Laura Numeroff (1985), meant more as a read-aloud than a read-alone and is a classic example of a chain of events that continually connects a series of actions to each other until the story again arrives at the beginning of the sequence. More current examples of the circular story create the same pattern with plenty of action, discernable illustrations, and repetitive yet unstilted language.

Laura Vaccaro Seeger has introduced the very basics of a circular story with her simple yet informative *First the Egg* (Roaring Brook, 2007). Three-word sentences matched by distinctly clear paintings explain the order of a number of things, bringing the reader full circle from egg to chicken to chicken to egg. In *One Boy* (Roaring Brook, 2008), she extends the circular concept through a brilliant display of word building and picture clues. Mary Serfozo's *Who Said Red?* (Margaret K. McElderry, 1988) employs the familiar theme of colors with rhyming text that weaves a number of repeated words in a variety of different color examples, always returning to the original question of the title. In *Blue Goose* (Simon & Schuster, 2008), Nancy Tafuri adds more

---

Circular Picture Books

Classics

Aliki. *At Mary Bloom's* (Greenwillow, 1976).

Nodset, Joan. *Who Took the Farmer's Hat?* (Harper & Row, 1963).

Numeroff, Laura. *If You Give a Mouse a Cookie* (Harper & Row, 1985).

Serfozo, Mary. *Who Said Red?* (Margaret K. McElderry, 1988).

Recent Gems

Seeger, Laura Vaccaro. *First the Egg* (Roaring Brook, 2007).

Seeger, Laura Vaccaro. *One Boy* (Roaring Brook, 2008).

Swanson, Susan Marie. *The House in the Night* (Houghton Mifflin, 2008).

Tafuri, Nancy. *Blue Goose* (Simon & Schuster, 2008).

---

vocabulary choices to a patterned sentence structure that returns to the title's namesake, Blue Goose. And in the 2009 Caldecott winner, *The House in the Night* (Houghton Mifflin, 2008), Susan Marie Swanson takes the basis of a simple cumulative pattern and interconnects all aspects of the house from the key, to the light, to the bed, to the book, to the bird and its song, bringing them full circle from outside to inside and back to outside the house at night.

Simple patterns in an easy-to-read text allow emerging and new readers to build confidence and word-recognition skills. Pattern picture books offer a text in which the basis of a sentence is repeated on each page with few alternate words to move the plot along. Examples of this are the infamous *The Carrot Seed* by Ruth Krauss (Harper & Row, 1945) and the longer *Mr. Gumpy's Outing* by John Burningham (Henry Holt, 1970). In David Martin's *All for Pie, Pie for All* (Candlewick, 2006), new readers have an opportunity to repeat each new version of the phrase several times before moving along in the story. And in Emma Garcia's *Tip Tip Dig Dig* (Boxer Books, 2007), children can repeat key words as they relate to the popular variety of trucks and construction vehicles.

Another pattern can be formed as a repeated question-and-answer exchange, such as Bill Martin's very successful *Brown Bear, Brown Bear, What Do You See?* (Henry Holt, 1983) and its sequels. Sue Williams in her similar *I Went Walking* (Harcourt Brace Jovanovich, 1989) follows a child's exploration of the animal world on his repetitive jaunt.

As in the above examples, a repeated phrase in a story encourages shared reading and helps develop fluency. Many predictable books incorporate a significant phrase within the story line, so its

Pattern Stories

Classics

Burningham, John. *Mr. Gumpy's Outing* (Henry Holt, 1970).

Hutchins, Pat. *The Doorbell Rang* (Greenwillow, 1986).

Hutchins, Pat. *Titch* (Macmillan, 1971).

Krauss, Ruth. *The Carrot Seed* (Harper & Row, 1945).

Recent Gems

Baddiel, Ivor. *Cock-A-Doodle Quack! Quack!* (David Fickling Books, 2007).

Baker, Keith. *Just How Long Can a Long String Be?!* (Arthur A. Levine/Scholastic, 2009).

Banks, Kate. *Fox* (Farrar, Straus and Giroux, 2007).

Butler, John. *If You See a Kitten* (Peachtree, 2002).

Butler, John. *Ten in the Meadow* (Peachtree, 2006).

Garcia, Emma. *Tip Tip Dig Dig* (Boxer Books, 2007).

Hillenbrand, Jane. *What a Treasure* (Holiday House, 2006).

MacDonald, Margaret Read. *A Hen, A Chick and a String Guitar* (Barefoot Books, 2005).

Martin, David. *All for Pie, Pie for All* (Candlewick, 2006).

Numeroff, Laura. *When Sheep Sleep* (Abrams, 2006).

Polacco, Patricia. *Mommies Say Shhh!* (Philomel, 2005).

Seeger, Laura Vaccaro. *Lemons Are Not Red* (Roaring Brook, 2004).

repetition produces an eager response from emerging and new readers. A wonderful example of this pattern is Michael Rosen's *We're Going on a Bear Hunt*, with two repetitive phrases separated by a newly introduced key phrase to further the plot. A simpler

Question-and-Answer Pattern

Classics

Carle, Eric. *Does A Kangaroo Have a Mother, Too?* (HarperCollins, 2000).

Kraus, Robert. *Whose Mouse are You?* (Macmillan, 1970).

Martin, Bill. *Brown Bear, Brown Bear, What Do You See?* (Henry Holt, 1983).

Williams, Sue. *I Went Walking* (Harcourt Brace Jovanovich, 1989).

Recent Gems

Butler, John. *Whose Nose and Toes?* (Viking, 2004).

Capucilli, Alyssa Satin. *What Kind of Kiss?* (HarperFestival, 2002).

Fox, Mem. *Where is the Green Sheep?* (Harcourt, 2004).

Thomas, Jan. *What Will Fat Cat Sit On?* Harcourt, 2007).

Van Laan, Nancy. *When Winter Comes* (Atheneum, 2000).

Repeated Phrase

Classics

Allen, Pamela. *Fancy That!* (Orchard Books, 1987).

Fleming, Denise. *Mamma Cat Has Three Kittens* (Henry Holt, 1998).

Fox, Mem. *Boo to a Goose* (Dial Books, 1998).

Hutchins, Pat. *Don't Forget the Bacon!* (Greenwillow, 1976).

Kalan, Robert. *Stop Thief!* (Greenwillow, 1993).

Plourde, Lynn. *Pigs in the Mud in the Middle of the Rud* (Blue Sky Press, 1997).

Rosen, Michael. *We're Going on a Bear Hunt* (Margaret K. McElderry Books, 1989).

Van Laan, Nancy. *So Say the Little Monkeys* (Atheneum, 1998).

Recent Gems

Capucilli, Alyssa Satin. *Little Spotted Cat* (Dial, 2005).

Fleming, Denise. *The Cow Who Clucked* (Henry Holt, 2005).

MacDonald, Margaret Read. *The Fat Cat* (August House/Little Folk, 2001).

Polacco, Patricia. *Oh, Look!* (Philomel Books, 2004).

Wilson, Karma. *Bear Snores On* (Margaret K. McElderry, 2002).

---

example of this story structure is *Boo to a Goose* by Mem Fox (Dial Books, 1998) with its consistent response to consecutive and droll rhyming verses.

The cumulative story allows emerging and new readers multiple opportunities to read the same sentences within one book. Of all the predictable story patterns, this one is the most common and easily available in picture book format, from *The House that Jack Built*, a classic Mother Goose rhyme retold by numerous illustrators and most notably by Simms Taback (Putnam, 2002), to variations like the latest by Pamela Edwards, *Jack and Jill's Treehouse* (Katherine Tegen Books, 2008), which builds its sentences around the construction of an elevated domain and offers picture cues in the form of a rebus.

Shared reading is also developed in classrooms with the use of short rhyming poems. Books that offer a sensible rhyming story pattern with words that can be easily anticipated as the story progresses provide new and emerging readers with opportunities to apply their prior language skills to phrases that make sense as they infer the meaning of the story. Teachers often use a "cloze activity" to have children fill in the blank as they listen; they are able to complete the verses themselves by supplying the order and sequence of the rhyming words.

Cumulative Stories

Classics

Fox, Mem. *Shoes from Grandpa* (Orchard Books, 1989).

Hogrogian, Nonny. *One Fine Day* (Macmillan, 1971).

Kalan, Robert. *Jump, Frog, Jump!* (Greenwillow, 1981).

McGovern, Ann. *Too Much Noise!* (Houghton Mifflin, 1967).

Tolstoy, Alexei. *The Great Big Enormous Turnip.* Helen Oxenbury, Illus (F. Watts, 1968).

Wood, Audrey. *The Napping House* (Harcourt Brace Jovanovich, 1984).

Recent Gems

Beil, Karen. *Jack's House* (Holiday House, 2008).

Clarke, Jane. *Stuck in the Mud* (Walker & Co., 2007).

Edwards, David. *The Pen That Pa Built* (Tricycle Press, 2007).

Edwards, Pamela. *Jack and Jill's Treehouse* (Katherine Tegen Books, 2008).

Lewis, Kevin. *My Truck is Stuck!* (Hyperion, 2002).

Nancy Shaw's *Sheep in a Jeep* (Houghton Mifflin, 1986) provides this sequence of rhyming opportunity simply with enough humorous action to warrant plenty of groans and laughs. Denise Fleming's paired wildlife settings *In the Tall, Tall Grass* (Henry Holt, 1991) and *In the Small, Small Pond* (Henry Holt, 1993) offer a string of more elegant and sophisticated rhyming sounds and words.

Rhyme Story Pattern

Classics

Florian, Douglas. *A Summer Day* (Greenwillow, 1998) and companion books, *A Beach Day* (1990) and *A Winter Day* (1987).

Garten, Jan. *The Alphabet Tale* (Greenwillow, 1994).

Shaw, Nancy. *Sheep in a Jeep* (Houghton Mifflin, 1986).

Williams, Sue. *Dinnertime!* (Harcourt, 2001).

Wood, Audrey. *Silly Sally* (Harcourt Brace Jovanovich, 1992).

Recent Gems

Anderson, Peggy Perry. *Chuck's Truck* (Houghton Mifflin, 2006) and *Chuck's Band* (2008).

Butler, John. *Can You Growl Like a Bear?* (Peachtree, 2007).

Elliott, David. *On the Farm* (Candlewick, 2008).

Gannij, Joan. *Hidden Hippo* (Barefoot Books, 2008).

Kuskin, Karla. *Under My Hood I Have a Hat* (HarperCollins, 2004).

MacLennan, Cathy. *Chicky Chicky Chook Chook* (Boxer Books, 2007).

Rosenthal, Amy Krouse. *It's Not Fair* (HarperCollins, 2008).

Shertle, Alice. *Little Blue Truck* (Harcourt, 2008).

Singing Rhymes

Classics

Galdone, Paul. *Cat Goes Fiddle-I-Fee* (Houghton Mifflin, 1985).

Langstaff, John. *Over in the Meadow* (Harcourt Brace Jovanovich, 1957).

Taback, Simms. *There Was an Old Lady Who Swallowed a Fly* (Viking, 1997).

Recent Gems

Baker, Keith. *Hickory Dickory Dock* (Harcourt, 2007).

Cabrera, Jane. *If You're Happy and You Know It!* (Holiday House, 2003).

Cabrera, Jane. *Over in the Meadow* (Holiday House, 1999).

Cabrera, Jane. *Ten in the Bed* (Holiday House, 2006).

Lloyd-Jones, Sally. *Old MacNoah Had an Ark* (HarperCollins, 2008).

Picture books created from familiar nursery rhymes and songs offer an excellent way to introduce this type of predictable singing rhyme book. John Langstaff's traditional *Over in the Meadow* (Harcourt Brace Jovanovich, 1957) and other more recent variations like *Over in the Garden* by Jennifer Ward (Rising Moon, 2002) encourage emerging readers to read and recite a familiar and repetitive text. Simms Taback's *There Was an Old Lady Who Swallowed a Fly* (Viking, 1997) adds the use of varied fonts, giving new readers an alternate view of printed text. And more recently, Jane Cabrera has produced a collection of familiar singing rhymes, each with a unique twist in the action.

Finally, the familiarity of easily recognizable sequence patterns such as days of the week, months in the year, numbers, and counting provide a facile and comfortable logic to a new reader's repertoire.

Sequence Pattern (Days of Week, Months, Numbers, etc.)

Classics

Carle, Eric. *Today is Monday* (Philomel, 1993).

Sendak, Maurice. *Chicken Soup with Rice* (Harper & Row, 1962).

Recent Gems

Baker, Keith. *Potato Joe* (Harcourt, 2008).

Darbyshire, Kristen. *Put It on the List!* (Dutton, 2009).

Denise, Anika. *Pig Love Potatoes* (Philomel Books, 2007).

Hayles, Marsha. *Pajamas Anytime* (Penguin Group, 2005).

Lies, Brian. *Bats at the Beach* (Houghton Mifflin, 2006).

Wood, Audrey. *Ten Little Fish* (Blue Sky Press/Scholastic, 2004).

Transitional Readers

As children transition from emerging to new readers, their confidence grows and their competence moves from recognizing patterns and predictable situations to developing intuitive comprehension abilities to make way for a new phase of reading material. Some of the characteristics and needs that Szymusiak and Sibberson (2001, 9) outlined for these readers include transitioning to more complicated and diverse story plots, genres, and formats with reading selections that move beyond the traditional easy reader or the I Can Read formula pioneered by Harper & Row.

One of the ways to maintain a comfort level between the predictable pattern picture book and a longer story that is not quite an early chapter book is to offer choices that provide several short story segments in either rhyme or prose within a very short anthology. A book such as Nancy Van Laan's *Teeny Tiny Tingly Tales* (Anne Schwartz/Atheneum, 2001) looks like and is shelved with the picture books, but is really a perfect example of such a short collection. Van Laan offers three rhyming short stories with enough repetition and rhyming wordplay for transitional readers to read both aloud and alone. They may stagger their pace by moving through the book one story per reading or all three at once. Whether reading all or part of the book, each story is short enough to achieve a feeling of completion. Jane Yolen provides easy rhyming versions of several Aesop tales in *A Sip of Aesop* (Blue Sky Press, 1995). And Mary Ann Hoberman, with her You Read to Me, I'll Read to You series, has created wonderful rhyming short story collections with color-coded text for shared read-alouds.

From rhyme to easy prose, Anne Rockwell's *Long Ago Yesterday* (Greenwillow, 1999) is a brief collection of two-page vignettes featuring real-life child-oriented situations. Doris Orgel's *The Lion & the Mouse and Other Aesop's Fables* (DK, 2000) uses large print and prose to bring out these classic tales. Laura Cecil in her compiled *Listen to This* (Greenwillow, 1987) is a treasure of thirteen easy-to-read folktales from classic authors such as Kipling, the Brothers Grimm, and Virginia Hamilton.

More commonly considered transitional books are the short chapter variety that offer several short episodic chapters or a short novel with an integrated and continual plot. These have been around for years, from Ann Cameron's Julian and Huey books (*The Stories Julian Tells* and *The Stories Huey Tells*), to the

---

Short Collections for Transitional Readers

Avi. *Things That Sometimes Happen* (Anne Schwartz/Atheneum, 2002).
Baumgartner, Barbara. *Crocodile, Crocodile: Stories Told Around the World* (DK, 1994).
Cecil, Laura. *Listen to This* (Greenwillow, 1987).
Hoberman, Mary Ann. *You Read to Me, I'll Read to You: Very Short Fairy Tales to Read Together* (Little, Brown, 2004).
Hoberman, Mary Ann. *You Read to Me, I'll Read to You: Very Short Mother Goose Tales to Read Together* (Little, Brown, 2005).
Hoberman, Mary Ann. *You Read to Me, I'll Read to You: Very Short Scary Tales to Read Together* (Little, Brown, 2007).
Hoberman, Mary Ann. *You Read to Me, I'll Read to You: Very Short Stories to Read Together* (Little, Brown, 2001).
Hoffman, Mary. *A Twist in the Tail* (Francis Lincoln, 2003).
Orgel, Doris. *The Lion & the Mouse and Other Aesop's Fables* (DK, 2000).
Rockwell, Anne. *Long Ago Yesterday* (Greenwillow, 1999).
Van Laan, Nancy. *Teeny Tiny Tingly Tales* (Anne Schwartz/Atheneum, 2001).
Yolen, Jane. *A Sip of Aesop* (Blue Sky Press, 1995).

---

familiar Cam Jansen mystery series by David Adler, to the newest boy *Stink*, sister to the invincible *Judy Moody*, created by Megan McDonald, to Lois Lowry's incredible Gooney Bird Greene books. These early chapter books sustain the thread of intrigue either with an episodic venue or full-length plot with which new readers can transition by either taking breaks between clearly defined episodes or chapters or choosing to reread their favorite parts multiple times.

The graphic novel publishing explosion has recently included the younger reader market with a newer, simplified, yet intriguing version of the popular format. Transitional readers familiar with the use of visual clues to interpret text from illustrated picture books or early chapter books can very easily migrate to more sophisticated reading through the sequencing and multiple literacy skills necessary for graphic novel reading. One of the first versions of a picture book in a graphic novel setting is Raymond Briggs's *Snowman* (Random House, 1978), whose story is told in a series of wordless panels.

Allyson Lyga, coauthor of *Graphic Novels in Your Media Center: A Definitive Guide* (Libraries Unlimited, 2004), reaffirms that the necessary comprehension skills for all reading are strengthened with the reading of graphic and practically wordless stories through the interpretation of sequence of events, characters' non-verbal gestures, discerning of story plot, and the making of inferences (Lyga 2009). Parents and teachers eager to move transitional readers from picture books to full text reading opportunities tend to lessen the importance of visual literacy skills that new readers are using to make meaning of their reading experiences. Unlike the accepted marriage of illustration and text for a well-crafted picture book, the graphic novel is somewhat misunderstood in its powerful ability to have transitional readers master their comprehension skills. Yet panel reading requires a more sophisticated interpretation of the story's plot, setting, and character development displayed through a connected series of images on a full page. The text can incorporate a variety of information that is offered through captions, dialogue, and thought balloons, making this type of reading more intricate. It can also include literary techniques such as flashbacks, irony, and symbolism that transitional readers are mastering.

The Theodore Seuss Geisel Honor Book, *Stinky* by Eleanor Davis (Toon, 2008), provides a wonderful example of a friendship story, full of pathos and charm with themes of good will and sympathetic humanity. Its well-designed series of panels and uncomplicated yet varied text allows transitional readers to work through the story's action and development while forming a sense of understanding about the similarities of the two very opposite main characters. John Lechner's heroic *Sticky Burr: Adventures in Burrwood Forest* (Candlewick, 2007) blends graphic novel conventions with traditional text and is another good choice for transitional readers.

Graphic Novels for Transitional Readers

Briggs, Raymond. *Ug* (Alfred A. Knopf, 2001).
Cammuso, Frank, and Jay Lynch. *Otto's Orange Day* (Toon, 2008).
Davis, Eleanor. *Stinky* (Toon, 2008).
Holm, Jennifer L., and Matthew Holm. *Babymouse: Queen of the World!* (Random House, 2005).
Feiffer, Jules. *Meanwhile …* (HarperCollins, 1997).
Lechner, John. *Sticky Burr: Adventures in Burrwood Forest* (Candlewick, 2007).
Pinkney, Brian. *The Adventures of Sparrowboy* (Simon, and Schuster, 1997).

There is an alternative format ever-present in novels, such as the highly popular Diary of a Wimpy Kid series by Jeff Kinney (Amulet Books) and Marissa Moss's *Amelia's Notebook* (Tricycle Press, 1995), which are a combination of traditional text and handwritten fonts in dual scrapbook and graphic novel presentations. These alternatives offer a plethora of visual and textual material to build on those visual literacy skills that are crucial to interpreting all the nuances of the story's plot and characters.

Struggling Readers

In looking for ways to reach out to a population of struggling and reluctant readers, the children's librarian's role is, in part, responsible for the recent shift in the way teachers and reading specialists have realigned their views on the use of graphic novels. There has also been a kind of mini-explosion in this field from educator-oriented graphic novel Web sites such as The Graphic Classroom Blog, written by librarian Michael Schofield (http://graphicclassroom.blogspot.com/), to a first conference "Graphica in Education: Graphic Novels Come Out from Under the Desk" hosted at Fordham University in January 2009. As with any new successful publishing format, publishers are delving more deeply into the school market and producing carefully crafted, well-designed products. And the National Council of Teachers of English has been paying attention as well, with an increase in their graphic novel conference programming.

The right introduction to a graphic novel can allow the struggling reader to focus on visual skills and to develop a basic understanding from the sequence of panels. This level of reading is crucial to building the necessary comprehension skills for good reading with meaning. Using a graphic novel with a majority of non-worded illustrations, such as in the Owly books by Andy Runton (Top Shelf) takes the edge off the stress a struggling reader may feel when concentrating on words rather than the "whole picture," if you will. Talking the story through with this reader to make sense of the action from the panels can enhance the comprehension strategies of prediction, prior knowledge, questioning and commenting, and the connections a reader can begin to make all from the visual imagery that is clearly evident.

From here, the struggling reader can retell, interpret, and infer meaning by discussing themes and character development gleaned through the artist's use of facial expressions, thought bubbles, and brief text. The heavy use of illustrative clues allows

---

Graphic Novels for Struggling or Reluctant Readers

Burleigh, Robert. *Into the Air: The Story of the Wright Brothers' First Flight* (Harcourt, 2002).
Huey, Debbie. *Bumperboy and the Loud, Loud Mountain* (Adhouse, 2006).
Huey, Debbie. *Bumperboy Loses His Marbles!* (Adhouse, 2005).
Kelly, John. *Wagon Train Adventure* (DK Graphic Readers, 2008).

---

the struggling reader to have that crucial mental conversation with the author so necessary for meaningful and enjoyable reading. Practicing these skills in a visual format that does not seem condescending for a second, third, or even older struggling or reluctant reader translates well to a more complicated text-driven format later on.

Teaching reluctant and struggling readers about literary techniques such as dialogue, point of view, flashbacks, and narrative style through visual and sequential art is another positive aspect of using graphic novels with this reader. Providing the reluctant reader with a graphic version of a particular book report assignment such as historical fiction or biography can offer a window of opportunity to encourage these children to read something they will be able to finish and respond to willingly.

Proficient Readers

What proficient yet complacent readers, as well as avid, eager readers have in common can be summed up in how they respond to their reading. In many of today's balanced literacy classrooms, much attention is paid to the theories of reader response. What children actually achieve or take away from their reading experiences has been interpreted most effectively by progressive educator Louise M. Rosenblatt (1982). Her groundbreaking "transactional theory of reading" identifies reading as a transaction between the reader and text. What this transaction achieves can be viewed from two different perspectives.

Rosenblatt refers to the Latin word *efferent*, which translates "to carry away," in order to explain the meaning or understanding a reader develops from the text (p. 269). Simultaneously, taking vocabulary from the Greek for "to sense" or "to perceive," Rosenblatt defines a reader's aesthetic response as the reader's emotional connections made with the text (p. 269). When a child reads, both responses, efferent or aesthetic, are not always equally present. Reading a nonfiction piece, such as how a seed grows into a plant, may trigger an understanding of the concept, while reading a literary piece such as a rap style poem may create a pleasing acceptance. If, however, the same child has experienced plant science by experimenting with her own seeds, her response to an informational book on plant science may elicit both an efferent and aesthetic response.

Rosenblatt's beliefs encourage reading instruction to evoke responses from both perspectives whenever possible. Reading instruction, in particular that of comprehension, teaches children to make the three connections—of text to self, text to text, and text to world—to attain responses that are efferent and aesthetic for a better, more satisfying, and interest-filled reading experience.

Dovetailing Literature-Based Library Programming with Reading Instruction

By cognitively incorporating many of the reading instructional principles of today's classrooms into your practice, you can greatly enhance your full-service youth library's programming. While we are not reading teachers, we are still educators and can be cognizant of how we structure our programming to create a follow-up or follow-through of what children are experiencing in their reading instruction. Remember, libraries are one of the three legs of education in a community, the other two being museums and schools (Soltan 2008, 26).

Story Time

When planning the variety of your story-hour sessions, be mindful of how storytelling and the choice of picture books can allow for greater participation from your young listeners. Select a broad variety of picture books so you will reach every reader. Incorporate alphabet recognition and rhyming pattern books to encourage emergent literacy skills and behaviors. Use predictable books within the traditionally theme-oriented plans to foster inference and meaning and develop listening and comprehension skills. For example, for a story time planned around a jungle animal theme, *The Alphabet Tale* by Jan Garten (Greenwillow, 1994) is a perfect book to introduce not only the letters of the alphabet, but comprehension skills through the question-and-answer, riddle-type rhyming text. Join this selection with the classic *Roar and More* by Karla Kuskin (Boyds Mills Press, 2004) and *Zoo-Looking* by Mem Fox (Mondo, 1996) for a "cloze" type participation activity. Finally, John Butler's *Can You Growl Like a Bear?* (Peachtree, 2007) offers little ones the opportunity to experience the various sounds of language as they listen and mimic.

Book Discussion

For transitional to older readers, broaden the concepts of book discussion through the use of interpretive questions that allow participants to make the three connections of text to self, text to text, and text to world that teachers often employ for comprehension. Work beyond the chosen book at hand to encourage readers to become more personally involved by connecting with their own experiences. For example, in Jeanne Birdsall's *The Penderwicks* (Random House, 2005), ask participants to relate their summer vacations and how adventurous their playtime can be. Make literacy connections with other similar books to compare with the discussion's selection and build on critical-thinking skills through compare-and-contrast exchanges. When discussing fairy tale versions, introduce three distinct interpretations of the traditional "three little pigs" scenario with James Marshall's straightforward telling in *The Three Little Pigs* (Dial, 1989), David Wiesner's pig-oriented adventurous escape in *The Three Little Pigs* (Clarion, 2001), and Jon Scieszka's wolf-explanatory narrative in *The True Story of the 3 Little Pigs!* (Viking, 1989). Ask your participants how these three versions stay and stray from the traditional telling and what makes each unique. Work with war-themed picture books like Dr. Seuss's *The Butter Battle Book* (Random, 1984) and Mem Fox's *Feathers and Fools* (Harcourt Brace, 1996) to explore some of the cultural divides in our current world. How do the similar themes and settings bring a higher level of awareness sparked by the books' overall messages?

Writing Activities

Develop a series of workshop-style programs that encourage writing. Build on the LEA instructional concept to encourage more early reading/writing story workshop sessions for younger grade students. Expand on this workshop idea by including readers' theater programming, allowing children to create their own scripts from existing favorite literature and even produce basic level puppet shows with simple paper bag puppets. Set up a group of series-style workshops, say for four-week sessions, to create more cohesive group activity on a regular basis and enforce the reading/writing connection crucial to developing strong reading skills.

Interactive Exhibits

Don't just focus on fiction, literature, and homework readers' advisory. Create nonfiction and specific subject matter opportunities, such as prehistory with dinosaurs, science, and invention. Use the summer months to create intriguing units and museum theme-type interactive displays that cultivate reading at a variety of levels. For ideas on this strategy, check out *Summer Reading Renaissance: An Interactive Exhibits Approach* (Libraries Unlimited, 2008).

Gaming

As with graphic novels, librarians have been on the forefront of new services, technologies, and reading experiences, including video and online gaming opportunities, thus advocating for alternate nontraditional forms of reading through technology. Gaming is now the hot ticket item in many 'tween and young adult library programs, which has resulted in some controversy in how it does or does not translate to reading and literacy behaviors. If we focus a bit on the play-to-learn connection, the use of traditional board games as well as the newer video and online game scenarios meld perfectly with other play-to-learn settings such as the learning centers so commonplace in today's constructivist-based classrooms.

Games encourage teamwork, critical-thinking skills, and a level of social interaction that molds interactive behaviors (Lipschultz 2009, 41). In addition, the visual component of a gaming situation can be an important tool in achieving some of the visual literacy so prominent in early reading experiences, as well as later ones with graphic novels. James Paul Gee, author of *What Video Games Have to Teach Us About Learning and Literacy* (Pargrave/Macmillan, 2007), points out that in our modern world of multiliteracies, the reading and writing connection must be accepted within different domains that communicate different meanings, not only through print, but through other symbolic and representational resources (p. 20). Good quality video and online games provide opportunity for active learning through experience or role playing, social affiliations through playing with others, the future ability to problem solve, and critical thinking by creative and innovative implementation (pp. 24–25).

Web Reading

Finally, "Web reading," whether it is a news article, a blog, an e-mail, or an instant message, is an alternate form of reading that our modern society has embraced. There are numerous ways to gather and obtain information as well as use reading skills for a variety of recreational pastimes. Teachers are concentrating more on the different literacy skills required to perform effective online researching. Children using search engines and even library purchased databases must learn to synthesize information from a wealth of choices that immediately pop up on the screen, not all related to their original keyword search. They must learn to sift through, skim, and discern good from inaccurate or incomplete information.

As librarians, we must remain cognizant of the differences and implications presented by traditional print over Internet publishing. In a recent *New York Times* article focusing on "the future of reading: digital versus print," Motoko Rich asserts "on paper, text has a predetermined beginning, middle, and end, where readers focus for a sustained period on one author's vision. On the Internet, readers skate through cyberspace at will, and, in effect, compose their own beginnings, middles, and ends" (Rich 2008, 14). How this alternate form of reading provides either an aesthetic or efferent response depends on what children are experiencing and are able to take away from all their reading efforts combined. The challenge for educators today is to address reading instruction from a multiliteracy perspective. Today's new literacies within a communications and technology environment are second nature to many children. But as proficient readers, they must combine foundational literacy skills of phonemic awareness, word recognition, decoding, vocabulary, comprehension, inferential reasoning, writing, spelling, and response to literature with the new media-oriented, image-rich software and Internet tools. In this sense, the terms "literacy" and "being literate" are continually redefined and evolving (Leu et al. 2004). The multiple focus of information that is provided over the Internet adds a new dimension to reading comprehension, which in some ways makes it more difficult to achieve the overall goal of "deep reading" or an "array of sophisticated processes that propel comprehension and that include inferential and deductive reasoning, analogical skills, critical analysis, reflection, and insight" (Wolf and Barzillai 2009). Teachers and librarians must concentrate more on the skills of reading critically to ascertain and discriminate the quality of text and information balanced against the reliability of the online source. One such avenue for deeper, more critically inferred reading is a well-designed WebQuest that offers a framework of instructional goals. Effective reading instruction will need to continually integrate the basic foundational skills with new and emerging literacies.

If literacy and the joy and satisfaction of reading are the major issues we advocate in our roles as children's librarians, promoting or coaching these initiatives must be encouraged through the family. Family literacy is crucial to a child's successful reading experiences.

References

Bishop, Kay, and Anthony Salveggi. "Responding to Developmental Stages in Reference Service to Children." *Public Libraries* 40, no. 6 (N/D 2001): 354–358.

Gee, James Paul. *What Video Games Have to Teach Us About Learning and Literacy.* New York: Pargrave/Macmillan, 2007.

Hart-Hewins, Linda, and Jan Wells. *Better Books! Better Readers!* York, ME: Stenhouse Publishers, 1999.

Leu, D. J., Jr., C. K. Kinzer, J. Coiro, and D. W. Cammack. "Toward a Theory of New Literacies Emerging from the Internet and Other Information and Communication Technologies." In R. B. Ruddell and N. Unrau (eds.), *Theoretical Models and Processes of Reading* (5th ed., pp. 1,570–1,613). Newark, DE: International Reading Association, 2004. Retrieved October 24, 2009, from http://www.readingonline. org/newliteracies/lit_index.asp?HREF=leu/.

Lipschultz, Dale. "Gaming @ Your Library." *American Libraries* (January/ February 2009): 40–43.

Lyga, Allyson A. W. "Graphic Novels for (Really) Young Readers." *School Library Journal* (March 3, 2009). Retrieved March 31, 2009, from http://www.schoollibraryjournal.com/article/CA6312463.html.

Rich, Motoko. "Literacy Debate: Online, R U Really Reading?" *New York Times,* July 27, 2008.

Rosenblatt, Louise M. "The Literary Transaction: Evocation and Response." *Theory into Practice* 21, no. 4, *Children's Literature* (Autumn 1982): 268–277.

Salvadore, Maria. "An Interview with Virginia A. Walter, Author of Children and Libraries: Getting It Right." *Journal of Youth Services in Libraries* 14, no. 3 (Spring 2001): 42–44.

Soltan, Rita. *Summer Reading Renaissance: An Interactive Exhibits Approach.* Westport, CT: Libraries Unlimited, 2008.

Wolf, Maryanne, and Mirit Barzillai. "The Importance of Deep Reading." *Educational Leadership* 66, no. 6 (March 2009): 32–37.

Children's Books Cited

Aliki. *At Mary Bloom's.* New York: Greenwillow, 1976.

Allen, Pamela. *Fancy That!* New York: Orchard Books, 1987.

Anderson, Peggy Perry. *Chuck's Truck.* New York: Houghton Mifflin, 2006, also *Chuck's Band* 2008.

Avi. *Things That Sometimes Happen.* New York: Anne Schwartz/Atheneum, 2002.

Baddiel, Ivor. *Cock-A-Doodle Quack! Quack!* Oxford; New York: David Fickling Books, 2007.

Baker, Keith. *Hickory Dickory Dock.* New York: Harcourt, 2007.

Baker, Keith. *Just How Long Can a Long String Be?!* New York: Arthur A. Levine/Scholastic, 2009.

Baker, Keith. *Potato Joe.* New York: Harcourt, 2008.

Banks, Kate. *Fox.* New York: Farrar, Straus and Giroux, 2007.

Baumgartner, Barbara. *Crocodile, Crocodile: Stories Told Around the World.* New York: DK, 1994.

Beil, Karen. *Jack's House.* New York: Holiday House, 2008.

Birdsall, Jeanne. *The Penderwicks.* New York: Random House, 2005.

Briggs, Raymond. *Ug.* New York: Alfred A. Knopf, 2001.

Burleigh, Robert. *Into the Air: The Story of the Wright Brothers' First Flight.* New York: Harcourt, 2002.

Burningham, John. *Mr. Gumpy's Outing.* New York: Henry Holt, 1970.

Butler, John. *Can You Growl Like a Bear?* Atlanta: Peachtree, 2007.

Butler, John. *If You See a Kitten.* Atlanta: Peachtree, 2002.

Butler, John. *Ten in the Meadow.* Atlanta: Peachtree, 2006.

Butler, John. *Whose Nose and Toes?* New York: Viking, 2004.

Cabrera, Jane. *If You're Happy and You Know It!* New York: Holiday House, 2003.

Cabrera, Jane. *Over in the Meadow.* New York: Holiday House, 1999.

Cabrera, Jane. *Ten in the Bed.* New York: Holiday House, 2006.

Cammuso, Frank, and Jay Lynch. *Otto's Orange Days.* New York: Toon, 2008.

Capucilli, Alyssa Satin. *Little Spotted Cat.* New York: Dial, 2005.

Capucilli, Alyssa Satin. *What Kind of Kiss?* New York: HarperFestival, 2002.

Carle, Eric. *Does A Kangaroo Have a Mother, Too?* New York: HarperCollins, 2000.

Carle, Eric. *Today is Monday.* New York: Philomel, 1993.

Cecil, Laura. *Listen to This*. New York: Greenwillow, 1987.

Clarke, Jane. *Stuck in the Mud*. New York: Walker & Co., 2007.

Darbyshire, Kristen. *Put It on the List!* New York: Dutton, 2009.

Davis, Eleanor. *Stinky*. New York: Toon, 2008.

Denise, Anika. *Pig Love Potatoes*. New York: Philomel Books, 2007.

Edwards, David. *The Pen That Pa Built*. Berkeley, CA: Tricycle Press, 2007.

Edwards, Pamela. *Jack and Jill's Treehouse*. New York: Katherine Tegen Books, 2008.

Elliott, David. *On the Farm*. Cambridge, MA: Candlewick, 2008.

Feiffer, Jules. *Meanwhile ...* New York: HarperCollins, 1997.

Fleming, Denise. *The Cow Who Clucked*. New York: Henry Holt, 2005.

Fleming, Denise. *Mamma Cat Has Three Kittens*. New York: Henry Holt, 1998.

Florian, Douglas. *A Summer Day*. New York: Greenwillow, 1998, also companion books, *A Beach Day*, 1990, and *A Winter Day*, 1987.

Fox, Mem. *Boo to a Goose*. New York: Dial Books, 1998.

Fox, Mem. *Feathers and Fools*. New York: Harcourt Brace, 1996.

Fox, Mem. *Shoes from Grandpa*. New York: Orchard Books, 1989.

Fox, Mem. *Where is the Green Sheep?* New York: Harcourt, 2004.

Fox, Mem. *Zoo-Looking*. Greenvale, NY: Mondo, 1996.

Gannij, Joan. *Hidden Hippo*. Cambridge, MA: Barefoot Books, 2008.

Galdone, Paul. *Cat Goes Fiddle-I-Fee*. New York: Houghton Mifflin, 1985.

Garcia, Emma. *Tip Tip Dig Dig*. London: Boxer Books, 2007.

Garten, Jan. *The Alphabet Tale*. New York: Greenwillow, 1994.

Hayles, Marsha. *Pajamas Anytime*. New York: Penguin Group, 2005.

Hillenbrand, Jane. *What a Treasure*. New York: Holiday House, 2006.

Hoberman, Mary Ann. *You Read to Me, I'll Read to You: Very Short Fairy Tales to Read Together*. New York: Little, Brown, 2004.

Hoberman, Mary Ann. *You Read to Me, I'll Read to You: Very Short Mother Goose Tales to Read Together*. New York: Little, Brown, 2005.

Hoberman, Mary Ann. *You Read to Me, I'll Read to You: Very Short Scary Tales to Read Together*. New York: Little, Brown, 2007.

Hoberman, Mary Ann. *You Read to Me, I'll Read to You: Very Short Stories to Read Together*. New York: Little, Brown, 2001.

Hoffman, Mary. *A Twist in the Tail*. New York: Francis Lincoln, 2003.

Hogrogian, Nonny. *One Fine Day*. New York: Macmillan, 1971.

Holm, Jennifer L., and Matthew Holm. *Babymouse: Queen of the World!* New York: Random House, 2005.

Huey, Debbie. *Bumperboy and the Loud, Loud Mountain*. Richmond, VA: Adhouse, 2006.

Huey, Debbie. *Bumperboy Loses His Marbles!* Richmond, VA: Adhouse, 2005.

Hutchins, Pat. *Don't Forget the Bacon!* New York: Greenwillow, 1976.

Hutchins, Pat. *The Doorbell Rang*. New York: Greenwillow, 1986.

Hutchins, Pat. *Titch*. New York: Macmillan, 1971.

Kalan, Robert. *Jump, Frog, Jump!* New York: Greenwillow, 1981.

Kalan, Robert. *Stop Thief!* New York: Greenwillow, 1993.

Kelly, John. *Wagon Train Adventure*. New York: DK Graphic Readers, 2008.

Kinney, Jeff. *Diary of a Wimpy Kid*. New York: Amulet Books, 2007.

Kraus, Robert. *Whose Mouse are You?* New York: Macmillan, 1970.

Krauss, Ruth. *The Carrot Seed*. New York: Harper & Row, 1945.

Kuskin, Karla. *Roar and More*. Honesdale, PA: Boyds Mills Press, 2004.

Kuskin, Karla. *Under My Hood I Have a Hat*. New York: HarperCollins, 2004.

Langstaff, John. *Over in the Meadow*. New York: Harcourt Brace Jovanovich, 1957.

Lechner, John. *Sticky Burr: Adventures in Burrwood Forest*. Cambridge, MA: Candlewick, 2007.

Lewis, Kevin. *My Truck is Stuck!* New York: Hyperion, 2002.

Lies, Brian. *Bats at the Beach*. New York: Houghton Mifflin, 2006.

Lloyd-Jones, Sally. *Old MacNoah Had an Ark*. New York: HarperCollins, 2008.

MacDonald, Margaret Read. *A Hen, a Chick and a String Guitar*. Cambridge, MA: Barefoot Books, 2005.

MacDonald, Margaret Read. *The Fat Cat*. Little Rock, AR: August House/ Little Folk, 2001.

MacLennan, Cathy. *Chicky Chicky Chook Chook*. London: Boxer Books, 2007.

Marshall, James. *The Three Little Pigs*. New York: Dial, 1989.

Martin, David. *All for Pie, Pie for All*. Cambridge, MA: Candlewick, 2006.

Martin, Bill. *Brown Bear, Brown Bear, What Do You See?* New York: Henry Holt, 1983.

McGovern, Ann. *Too Much Noise!* New York: Houghton Mifflin, 1967.

Moss, Marissa. *Amelia's Notebook*. Berkeley, CA: Tricycle Press, 1995.

Nodset, Joan. *Who Took the Farmer's Hat?* New York: Harper & Row, 1963.

Numeroff, Laura. *If You Give a Mouse a Cookie*. New York: Harper & Row, 1985.

Numeroff, Laura. *When Sheep Sleep*. New York: Abrams, 2006.

Orgel, Doris. *The Lion & the Mouse and Other Aesop's Fables*. New York: DK, 2000.

Pinkney, Brian. *The Adventures of Sparrowboy*. New York: Simon & Schuster, 1997.

Plourde, Lynn. *Pigs in the Mud in the Middle of the Rud*. New York: Blue Sky Press, 1997.

Polacco, Patricia. *Mommies Say Shhh!* New York: Philomel, 2005.

Polacco, Patricia. *Oh, Look!* New York: Philomel Books, 2004.

Rockwell, Anne. *Long Ago Yesterday.* New York: Greenwillow, 1999.

Rosen, Michael. *We're Going on a Bear Hunt.* New York: Margaret K. McElderry Books, 1989.

Rosenthal, Amy Krouse. *It's Not Fair.* New York: HarperCollins, 2008.

Runton, Andy. *Owly.* Marietta, GA: Top Shelf, 2004.

Scieszka, Jon. *The True Story of the 3 Little Pigs!* New York: Viking, 1989.

Serfozo, Mary. *Who Said Red?* New York: Margaret K. McElderry, 1988.

Seeger, Laura Vaccaro. *First the Egg.* New Milford, CT: Roaring Brook, 2007.

Seeger, Laura Vaccaro. *Lemons Are Not Red.* New Milford, CT: Roaring Brook, 2004.

Seeger, Laura Vaccaro. *One Boy.* New Milford, CT: Roaring Brook, 2008.

Sendak, Maurice. *Chicken Soup with Rice.* New York: Harper & Row, 1962.

Seuss, Dr. *The Butter Battle Book.* New York: Random, 1984.

Shaw, Nancy. *Sheep in a Jeep.* New York: Houghton Mifflin, 1986.

Shertle, Alice. *Little Blue Truck.* New York: Harcourt, 2008.

Simms Taback. *There Was an Old Lady Who Swallowed a Fly.* New York: Viking, 1997.

Swanson, Susan Marie. *The House in the Night.* New York: Houghton Mifflin, 2008.

Tafuri, Nancy. *Blue Goose.* New York: Simon & Schuster, 2008.

Thomas, Jan. *What Will Fat Cat Sit On?* New York: Harcourt, 2007.

Tolstoy, Alexei. *The Great Big Enormous Turnip.* Helen Oxenbury, Illus. New York: F. Watts, 1968.

Van Laan, Nancy. *So Say the Little Monkeys.* New York: Atheneum, 1998.

Van Laan, Nancy. *Teeny Tiny Tingly Tales.* New York: Anne Schwartz/Atheneum, 2001.

Van Laan, Nancy. *When Winter Comes.* New York: Atheneum, 2000.

Wiesner, David. *The Three Little Pigs.* New York: Clarion, 2001.

Williams, Sue. *Dinnertime!* New York: Harcourt, 2001.

Williams, Sue. *I Went Walking.* New York: Harcourt Brace Jovanovich, 1989.

Wilson, Karma. *Bear Snores On.* New York: Margaret K. McElderry, 2002.

Wood, Audrey. *The Napping House.* New York: Harcourt Brace Jovanovich, 1984.

Wood, Audrey. *Silly Sally.* New York: Harcourt Brace Jovanovich, 1992.

Wood, Audrey. *Ten Little Fish.* New York: Blue Sky Press/Scholastic, 2004.

Yolen, Jane. *A Sip of Aesop.* New York: Blue Sky Press, 1995.

CHAPTER 5

Family Reading Coach

One of the first assignments in the MAT in reading and language arts program was to trace my personal family literacy history. I was the child of immigrant parents with limited English skills and little knowledge of the benefits of reading to children and exposing them to books at a very young age. Without any organized English-language learner program available then (the early 1950s), I entered kindergarten and first grade with great fear, immediately realizing I had a problem understanding the teacher. Somehow I managed to learn my letters, sounds, and to read, totally immersed in this sink-or-swim environment. I don't really remember how this actually happened, only that school for the first few years was a struggle, and I knew I had to work harder than the others to succeed.

My childhood experience with immigrant parents who were limitedly involved in my reading instruction influenced me to understand the importance of reading aloud to kids as early as possible. As a parent and as a professional, it has been my mantra to encourage, as much as possible, reading as part of regular, daily family time. Early pre-reading literacy activities are an important part of the everyday experiences of babies and preschoolers so that they are conditioned to be ready and eager to continue their informal exposure to reading in a more formal way at school with, hopefully, positive results. And more importantly, parents need to continue reading aloud to their children after the children are reading themselves, to further the benefits of sharing good literature together.

Literacy researchers, experts, and teachers recognize and agree that a child's reading and school success directly correlates to the literacy behaviors prevalent in his or her home. Family literacy, a phrase coined in recent years, can be defined in different ways and has different levels of significance based on a child's socioeconomic environment. Children today are raised in a broad range of home situations beyond the traditional nuclear family household— from single parent to grandparent to teen parent to immigrant parent. While many of these caregivers possess literacy skills and some hold higher levels of education, how families incorporate reading with their children into their everyday lives provides the critical link between family literacy and a child's reading achievement.

How is reading brought into the home? Is reading limited to the daily newspaper or Web sites and blogs for the adults in the household, or are children's books shared and explored on a habitual basis? Is emergent literacy encouraged through play, or just limited to the cleverly created scenarios developed for our well-crafted educational television programming? And of course, are library visits a regular routine, like the weekly grocery shopping? For many families struggling with poverty and life's chaos, these questions never even come up on their radar screen. Librarians must be on the forefront with community and early childhood agencies to make reading and literacy an essential and pleasing experience embedded within each family's daily lifestyle by providing guidance, encouragement, enthusiasm, and inspiration—in other words, by taking on the role of a coach in regular family reading initiatives.

Family reading is an activity that spans a wide range of opportunities beyond the traditional bedtime story or read-aloud session most prevalent in middle-class homes. For homes where literacy is limited or illiteracy prevails, the challenge is to find ways to provide the necessary coaching—most notably beyond the library's walls. This challenge has been undertaken in numerous ways with the efforts of local literacy councils, federal and state early childhood agencies, government humanities programs, and the American Library Association. In the last decade, many libraries have done a remarkable job of tapping into and collaborating with these efforts to promote greater family literacy and reading initiatives.

Head Start, "the longest running, national school readiness program in the United States, provides comprehensive education, health, nutrition, and parent involvement services to low-income children and their families" (http://www.nhsa.org/about_nhsa), while Even Start, a newer initiative begun in 1992, "supports family literacy services for parents with low literacy skills or who have limited English proficiency, and their children, primarily birth through age seven including teen parents" (http://www.ed.gov/programs/evenstartformula/index.html). FACE, or Family and Child Education, was developed in 1990 and "designed as a family literacy program—an early childhood/parent involvement program for American Indian families in schools funded by the Bureau of Indian Education. [It] provides culturally responsive education, resources, and support for American Indian families to better prepare American Indian children for school" (http://www.leschischools.org/support/familyed.php).

More recently, the award-winning Prime Time Family Reading program concentrates on children between the ages of six and ten and their families with a six-to-eight-week series blending book discussion on humanities themes and storytelling with demonstrations of effective read-aloud techniques. Initiated in Louisiana, it encompasses the library by allowing "librarians to introduce families to library resources, such as other books, homework aids, ESL and GED materials for parents, books on parenting and healthcare, and local and international newspapers and magazines." The primary goal of this uniquely designed program is that it "transforms families into lifelong readers [and] creates the precondition for all learning and helps to end the cycle of intergenerational illiteracy" (http://www.leh.org/html/primetime.html).

Every Child Ready to Read @ Your Library, a combined partnership between the Public Library Association, the Association of Library Service to Children, and the National Institute of Child Health and Human Development, has had a very significant impact on training parents and caregivers as first teachers in emergent literacy skills and behaviors. By building on the traditional story time sessions, librarians incorporate and add parent workshops that stress child literacy development and introduce a series of successful and research-based emergent literacy concepts as part of story reading.

All of these programs are strong examples of what is being done on a national level to encourage and promote family literacy. However, coaching requires a more localized, concerted effort to reach out and work with families throughout the community.

Dovetailing Reading Instruction with Family Reading Initiatives

Everything you do as a children's librarian serving a community of families is rooted in literacy. What needs to be added to the pot of family reading initiatives is a cognizant approach to reading instruction rationale that helps prime a child for literacy through the basic child-development stages of

- learning language through talking and listening,
- learning social and emotional behaviors through play, and
- learning about written language through the various stages of reading (from emergent to beginning to reading).

Children's librarians are charged with helping parents and caregivers understand that learning to talk, play, read, and write creates a powerful interconnection to literacy development.

Fostering Literacy Development Through Language, Play, and Reading

Learning Language

We know that before young children learn to talk, they accomplish the amazing task of learning to communicate through sounds, facial expressions, and body language. Developing their language and speaking ability by listening to and imitating sounds and words provides a foundation for toddlers' and young preschoolers' future reading success. Helping parents recognize their strengths as first teachers in their children's language development can be the core of this approach. This may be achieved through the implementation of programming that addresses both parent and child, as well as in parent-only workshops.

Design parent and child story hours and open literacy play sessions to foster the importance of talking with baby, toddler, and preschooler. Help parents and caregivers understand that conversation, however basic and elementary, coupled with books is the foundation for early literacy development. For example, a story hour and/or parent workshop can be built around the three stages of language development, from a baby's babble to a toddler's chatter of beginning sounds and early small words to a preschooler's sprouting combination of words and brief sentences. Incorporating key language-development factors within the story session or workshop demonstration helps parents, especially those with limited literacy or English knowledge, know that their greatest strength—simply talking with their baby, toddler, and preschooler—can be the crux of literacy development. Some basic facts to point out to parents include:

- Babies learn to talk when parents and adults talk to their babies.
- Babbling, gurgles, coos, and grunts are important first verbal steps in speaking.
- Between six and nine months, babies begin to hear and repeat certain consonant/vowel sounds, like "da-da" or "ma-ma."
- Between nine and twelve months, babies can understand very simple words.
- Between twelve and fifteen months, babies begin to say simple words as they connect words with meaning.
- Between fifteen and eighteen months, babies use words and gestures, like pointing, to communicate.
- Between eighteen and twenty-four months, babies can understand directions and make simple two-word sentences, like "Mama up."
- Between twenty-four and thirty-six months, babies' language takes a leap by knowing and using more words to form longer sentences, questions, and answers.

Highlighting how listening leads to the imitating of sounds and how the sounds of language make up the words and sentences of communication reinforces the importance of talking to and with the youngest. Finally, explaining how children three years old and older learn to manipulate sounds by

- forming nonsensical words—adding or removing sounds—fee, fi, fo, fum;
- rhyming words—bat, cat, rat;
- segmenting or taking words apart to the smallest individual sounds—b-a-t; and
- blending sounds to make words—oom, room, broom.

can introduce the idea of phonological awareness as the forerunner of a child's reading development. This is not to say that your story hours and programming should be filled with pedagogical directives. Rather, inserting a few gentle reminders or points throughout the sessions and including a handout each week with follow-up suggestions for similar books related to the day's theme or even a bookmark style giveaway with some of the pointers listed below will help pass along the message. Another way is to converse individually with your parents and caregivers, with a well-intentioned question here and there about their choices and interests in book selection and read-aloud time at home.

Activities to encourage with parents and caregivers for language development:

Foster Language Development with Your Child

- Sing and say nursery rhymes.
- Converse with baby; listen to his or her babbling and respond with words.
- Encourage baby to repeat simple words as you describe his or her actions.
- Describe what baby and you both see and do.
- Add to your child's commentary, however basic.
- Keep the conversation going by asking questions and eliciting answers.

Concepts to encourage with parents and caregivers for language growth through read-aloud sessions:

Reading to Your Child Fosters Language Growth

- Your child's listening potential can be higher than his or her reading potential.
- Your child begins to distinguish between spoken and written language.
- Your child is exposed to new words and more complex vocabulary.
- Your child's listening skills enhance comprehension skills.
- Read-alouds provide a base for imaginative and critical thinking.
- Read-alouds provide a base for social and behavior development through thematic situations.

Learning Through Play

Young children's play helps them observe, explore, experiment, investigate, and construct meaning about their surroundings. Play offers opportunities to develop and practice social, emotional, intellectual, and physical skills.

Play Development

- Babies are naturally inquisitive and play by using their senses. They look at and point, listen to different sounds, grab, touch, and even try to taste whatever they can place in their mouths.
- Young toddlers are able to play with age-appropriate toys designed for easy manipulation. They begin to use toys or objects to imitate real life, like telephone conversations.
- Older toddlers are able to create pretend play situations using their imagination. Pretend play helps the child begin to use language skills to talk about what he is doing or act out a pretend role.
- Preschoolers invent more complex play by connecting one activity to another. Play becomes more social as they learn to communicate and relate to peers, siblings, and adults.

Play and Language Development

- Singing and making up rhymes with a child introduces the rhythm, cadence, and sounds of language.
- Talking about everyday occurrences and routines introduces new words for rich vocabulary.
- New words provide opportunities to learn new sounds and pronunciation.
- Explaining and describing play activity introduces sequence.
- Asking open-ended questions builds thinking skills and encourages new ideas.

Play and the Reading Connection

- Children's play helps develop new language skills, a precursor to reading.
- Providing books in the play environment encourages children's exploration of reading materials equal to that of their toys.

- Books and reading aloud models good reading behaviors. Children learn how to hold a book, turn pages, react to words and pictures, and tell or "pretend read" a story.
- Talking about books and their stories and illustrations helps children understand and describe by retelling or repeating key words and phrases in the story.

Activities to encourage with parents and caregivers for play development:

Baby Play

- Give baby simple objects, like a rattle, that he or she can hold, shake, drop, and experiment.
- Imitate baby's actions and facial expressions.
- Play lap-sit games like peekaboo and row your boat.

Child Play

- Encourage imaginative play with basic objects and simple toys.
- Join in and interact with your child and his or her playing.
- Provide puzzles and manipulative toys like blocks to encourage cognitive skills.
- Provide paper, crayons, and pencils to encourage early scribbling and writing.
- Let your child lead, but also guide him or her with concrete directions.

Learning to Read

Children develop reading skills in three stages. Reviewing some of the basic tasks for each stage—emergent, beginning, and reading—we explored in earlier chapters, can help to outline some of the suggestions for parents and caregivers.

The Emergent Stage—Before actual reading happens, toddlers and preschoolers display a variety of *emerging reading tasks*. Emergent readers

- communicate through speech with a basic level of understanding,

- understand letters have certain sounds,
- identify most letters of the alphabet with their corresponding sounds,
- begin to see words are made up of combined sounds,
- understand that words are printed on a page with a combination of letters,
- understand printed words have a message or story to tell,
- understand pictures and words help tell a story,
- play with language through rhyming games,
- accept reading as another form of enjoyable daily activity,
- are increasingly interested in repeated readings of the same book and new offerings each day, and
- imitate writing with their own scribbling.

The Beginning Stage—Reading is actually taking place in small limited ways as children develop these *beginning reading tasks*. Beginning readers

- can retell a very familiar story using many words from the text,
- can describe the story from the illustrations,
- can visually recognize some letter/sound combinations,
- understand rhyming concepts and beginning sounds in words,
- can sort words by sound combinations,
- understand reading happens from top to bottom and left to right,
- can begin to memorize and recognize some very frequently used words, and
- can write the alphabet and their name.

The Reading Stage—Reading is more fluent, flexible, and thoughtful. Children can read at a level that is *independently comfortable* and perform these more *advanced reading tasks*.

Fluent readers

- read a sentence or passage automatically because they recognize all the words,
- break down new and more difficult words by using letter/sound combinations,
- self-correct reading errors based on context or meaning,

- add new words to their bank of vocabulary more frequently,
- reread or retell with ease and expression,
- use certain strategies if they get stuck or if they do not understand,
- make predictions about what they are going to read from the title and pictures,
- develop interest in a combination of formats—stories and information books,
- form questions about what they have read,
- write simple sentences related to what they have read or experienced, and
- begin to understand punctuation marks and the use of capitalization.

This stage continues to develop throughout a child's life as they move further into more complex reading materials and develop greater comprehension skills and reading interests.

The Reading and Writing Connection

Language Experience Stories and Activities

As mentioned previously, writing adds another venue to accomplishing reading success. A child's personal story can also be written either by the child, parent, or teacher. Children who are encouraged to write their own stories, either alone or with an adult, are more easily able to make the connection to reading. Reading *their* stories with *their* words makes learning to read more accessible. Children learn that *spoken words can be written and written words can be read.*

Concepts to encourage with parents and caregivers for reading development:

Reading with Your Baby and Toddler

- Use simple board books with large colorful pictures.
- Point and talk about what you see.
- Let baby point and turn pages when she is ready.
- Build up reading time; start with five minutes and graduate to twenty.

Reading with Your Preschooler and Early Elementary Child

- Set up a routine time each day for reading and sharing books together.
- Use eyes for expression—happy, sad, shock, surprise.
- Use voice for contrast—loud or soft, fast or slow, high or low.
- Talk about the story and pictures together.
- Ask your child to predict what might happen in the story.
- Retell the story together.
- Read favorites each day and at least one new story each week.
- Keep a family journal to record stories together.

Family Reading Road Show

Embedding the above concepts and principles within your library's routine family and child programming is one way of providing some coaching. But what is really needed is a series of demonstrations and workshops brought to places outside the library, such as:

- child care agency training sessions
- community college child care degree classes
- parent awareness meetings at hospitals
- community centers
- religious venues

This outreach helps encourage families to include literacy opportunities in the home and to use the library's resources more regularly. This kind of coaching requires a road show for the widest distribution that can be reinforced with partnering efforts created with local experts such as speech therapists, reading specialists, or early childhood professors who are willing to lend a supporting hand to this worthy initiative.

Check out the following organizations for additional ideas on language development, play, and family reading initiatives:

National Association for the Education of Young Children
http://www.naeyc.org/

ZERO TO THREE
http://www.zerotothree.org/

The Importance of Family Literacy Coaching

As an active role model in supporting family literacy, you as a librarian can engage in two interrelated objectives, that of developing an understanding of the basics of literacy behaviors for parents and caregivers, and that of enhancing reading interests and skills for both adults and children within their home environment. Combining mediums of talk, play, and reading within a relaxed home atmosphere takes the learning aspect of literacy instruction beyond the classroom. Encouraging conversation about favorite books and stories, maintaining a family book collection through personal purchases, and, of course, library borrowing, as well as elevating reading and discussing together as an enjoyable daily escape from the school and workday can make the critical difference between struggling and successful readers and students.

Resources

Even Start http://www.ed.gov/programs/evenstartformula/index.html

Every Child Ready to Read @ Your Library A joint project of the Public Library Association and the Association of Library Service to Children http://www.ala.org/ala/mgrps/divs/alsc/ecrr/index.cfm

Family and Child Education (FACE) http://www.leschischools.org/support/familyed.php

Louisiana Endowment for the Humanities Prime Time Family Reading Time http://www.leh.org/html/primetime.html

National Association for the Education of Young Children http://www.naeyc.org/

National Head Start Association http://www.nhsa.org/about_nhsa

ZERO TO THREE http://www.zerotothree.org/

CHAPTER 6

Partner with Educators

Several years ago, I led a daylong workshop on incorporating book discussion programming within middle and high school English and social studies curriculums. The workshop had been organized by the school district's libraries coordinator, who had also invited the school librarians to participate. As I addressed my audience, I unconsciously thought of the group as fellow librarians and openly referred to them as such during my opening remarks. By the end of the first hour, a participant raised her hand and informed me in no uncertain terms, "We are ALL teachers here." She was a bit indignant, as if to imply that the term "librarian" did not apply to this group, that in some way it invoked a lesser profession, and that they were to be considered equal to that of the teaching staff.

I was taken aback by the immediate consensus of the group and quickly recovered in order to explain that "teacher-librarian" was what we all understood our roles to be. What I later learned was that this district had just endured a long union fight to include librarians in the teaching contract as equal professionals, and that the title of librarian had a history of creating a lesser status on the pay scale and in the bargaining agreement.

Of the many roles you play as a librarian, the one that sometimes tends to offer differing sets of criteria and definitions is that of educator. Over the years I have heard statements such as, "librarians are not teachers" and "teachers instruct but librarians guide." School media specialists have also been expected to incorporate media and technology in their role, thus their non-librarian sounding title. Yet, in many ways, we all play a part in instruction as we teach our patrons, students, and classes how to research, create reports and presentations, and build on literacy skills through a wealth of reading opportunities. And when it comes to reading instruction, our goals are clearly the same—to encourage lifelong reading that is skillful and provides interactive, meaningful, and pleasurable experiences. To that end, you must create an environment that focuses on collaboration with your school colleagues, partnering with them to create effective reading instructional methods and support systems. As a librarian, you must be proactive in letting your school colleagues have a clear understanding of the contribution you make to those goals.

Sharing the Instructional Landscape

The divisions created within school buildings and between schools, schools and public libraries, and other community agencies develop from a continual tug and pull of instructional territory. Teachers feel the pressure of providing measureable results, often solely indicated through rigid standardized testing. While they may appreciate outside support systems, consider their limited time constraints to achieve those mandated outcomes. Rightly so, teachers are on the front lines of providing effective reading instruction. Yet sharing this responsibility with collaborative efforts through the various support systems beyond their classrooms and buildings can prove to be that much more successful in developing a complete and balanced reading program.

As educators, librarians must present themselves as colleagues working to improve reading instruction goals. The resistance often comes from the teacher's perspective, assuming that the librarian has a different perception or no clear concept of the reading instruction philosophy and strategies. Clarifying this misinterpretation is vital to initiating collaboration between teachers and librarians. Teachers need to feel that their efforts and time spent in a collaborative environment will result in a worthwhile cohesive blending of instruction and support. Librarians must communicate effectively to demonstrate their knowledge of the reading program and offer ways to incorporate their services consistent with the school's pedagogical requirements. Each must leave the trusted enclave of the classroom and library to work together through a series of networking opportunities to develop a reliable and productive plan of action. One way to begin is through an initial summit at the beginning of each school year.

The Summit

The beginning of the school year can be both an exciting new start as well as a time of rethinking past methods, plans, and ideas. Classroom teachers are extremely busy at this time, getting ready for the new term, setting up classrooms, and developing and reworking lesson plans. At the same time, administrators are busy planning and leading welcome-back-faculty meetings. Parent-teacher organizations (PTOs) are scheduling and recruiting members for fundraising and supportive programs. While all three groups seem to be working separately, a way to bring everyone together for a reintroduction to the public and school library's role in the reading program is to jointly host, with the school media specialist, a welcome-back early morning breakfast summit of key leaders.

Invite PTO board members, school administrators, reading specialists, and other support staff and highlight reading instruction as the major focus of the meeting. This is a kind of summit where leaders with different perspectives can come together to provide a more complete picture of what and how reading instruction can be enhanced and improved with all the various resources available throughout the district and the community. The summit also offers an opportunity to explain the supportive and crucial role everyone plays in recognizing the library's key purpose—that of providing access to reading instructional support.

Getting the leaders on board first makes it easier for the classroom teachers to grow and achieve through this kind of collaboration as the message is related back to the faculty on the front lines of reading instruction. Leaders converge to explore ways to bring all players to the field for a new school year where reading instruction is the focus of all other successful learning, with effective participation both in and outside the classroom setting. Teachers, already stressed to the limit, can be encouraged by the benefits of working together and learning about the roles and responsibilities of support players in the community and what can be shared for the sake of providing the most complete reading instruction. Librarians can take the steps to be coordinators in this effort, rather than a twenty-minute guest of the school district once or twice a year at a faculty meeting or assembly visit. The goal is to encourage a series of networking, knowledge-sharing efforts comprised of members across the educational community, each with an interest or expertise in reading instruction. Another way to think of this is in terms of communities of practice.

Communities of Practice

Organizational philosophy has for several years included the concept of networking to share goals and visions of a particular idea or plan. The concept of communities of practice (CoP) is one that was born out of the research that Etienne Wenger, Richard McDermott, and William Snyder incorporated on learning and performance measures within organizational structures. Individuals working in the same or related fields of interest can expand and extend their knowledge through a communal social structure that is designed to informally create knowledge-based connections. Wenger, McDermott, and Snyder define CoPs as "groups of people who share a concern, a set of problems, or a passion about a topic, and who deepen their knowledge and expertise in this area by interacting on an ongoing basis" (Wenger, McDermott, and Snyder 2002, 4).

Many of us, either through our work environment or outside it, interact regularly with communities or groups with related interests. You may meet regularly with fellow children's librarians within your library cooperative or your library system for programming ideas, collection resources, and so on. You may be part of a discussion group outside of work with a particular interest or focus on certain genres. You may volunteer in some capacity with a local literacy group. Or you may be active or just a bystander absorbing knowledge through a professional organization. What a CoP emphasizes is the ability to manage the knowledge that is being shared within a socialized venue. In today's organizational world, CoPs are a common and natural phase of knowledge sharing, crucial to gaining greater productivity and successful outcomes. Each CoP includes three basic components:

- a *domain* or common ground or identity
- a *community* wherein learning takes place through a socialized venue fostering respect and trust
- a *practice* that might include a framework of tools, ideas, information, styles, language, and stories that community members share with each other (Wenger, McDermott, and Snyder 2002, 27–29)

Within the educational community of a neighborhood, town, or city, the school district is at the center surrounded by various related groups or agencies. These groups and agencies can be university professors, college education majors, museum educators, librarians, early childhood agencies, day care directors, psychologists, parents, and even local bookstores or child-oriented businesses. In other words, the school in any community does not operate in a vacuum. It is an integral part of the entire surrounding educational community that plays a role in the learning process of children and families. There are numerous possibilities throughout the entire educational community of a town to create CoPs for literacy and reading instruction. These possibilities are dependent on how each of these related groups and agencies may:

- Consider ways to interact and come together for a common identity or purpose.
- Meet in various ways to introduce and share their expertise and knowledge.
- Demonstrate or relate various ideas, methods, and practices.

In her book *The School Buddy System: The Practice of Collaboration*, Gail Bush focuses on the many ways that educators in an educational community can leave their individual areas of expertise to come together "in a quest for goal-oriented, purposeful educator collaboration" (Bush 2003, 93). Taking cues from the constructivist teaching approach employed in many classrooms today, CoP opportunities offer collaborative learning and working relationships. Each group of professionals and participants in the school and surrounding agencies and organizations has something to gain by learning from one another and in concert with each other.

For example, one of the most powerful ways to achieve this is through the built-in school community of parents and faculty. Parent-teacher organizations offer librarians a doorway into the school's arena. Librarians interact with parents on a daily basis and frequently communicate with the PTO's administrative body. This administrative body continually interacts with the school's faculty and administration and is often influential in the outside support it sponsors. School administrators use the PTO's influence to plan and execute effective parent informational meetings regarding instructional goals and outcomes. A collaborative model includes a reading instruction support system that joins participation from parents, teachers, and librarians in a CoP. This requires foresight and planning, with the long-term goals that align the interests of parents, teachers, and librarians to help children become competent lifelong readers.

Different CoPs Have Different Goals

Wegner, McDermott, and Snyder outline four categories of CoPs that might develop around one common interest (Wegner, McDermott, and Snyder 2002, 76). The first are "helping communities" that are formed in order to solve problems by disseminating good ideas across organizations or agencies and identifying new practices. The second are "best-practice communities" where the focus is on developing, validating, and disseminating specific practices and verifying the effectiveness and benefits of existing practices. The third are "knowledge-stewarding communities" that seek to organize, upgrade, and distribute knowledge that community members use every day. And lastly, there are "innovation communities" that foster unexpected ideas and innovations in the same way as "helping communities" but intentionally cross boundaries to mix members from differing groups and organizations.

One way to begin this learning process is through professional national associations. Committee involvement and responsibilities are a normal part of professional life. Many teachers and librarians participate in state and national associations that target either the teaching or the librarian profession. Forming a local CoP with representation from the various support groups and agencies creates "knowledge-stewarding" communities within the immediate educational community. These CoPs can target ways to bring the educational community together through approaches from different venues that strengthen reading instruction.

The American Library Association and its children's and school's related divisions, the Association for Library Service to Children (ALSC), and the American Association of School Librarians (AASL), have established committees, blogs, and even online courses related to reading and instructional strategies. Similarly, teachers and, in particular, reading specialists benefit greatly through their participation with the International Reading Association (IRA). The IRA provides support to anyone interested in literacy education through its many publications, professional communities, conferences, and events.

A CoP of local librarians and teachers who are active in any of the above associations can cross boundaries by choosing to attend certain functions or to even just explore Web sites and online publications from these national organizations. For example, the IRA offers a section on "advocacy and outreach" on its Web site (http://www.reading.org/General/Legislative.aspx) and (http://www. reading.org/Resources/ResourcesByTopic.aspx), with links to numerous special interest groups such as "adult education and family literacy," "children's literature and reading," and "storytellers." While membership is required, participation adds to a librarian's learning curve in terms of reading instruction. At the same time, encouraging the teaching profession to glean information from library associations adds to their knowledge of how we provide support. State and regional associations reflecting both library service and reading initiatives provide localized professional support and a greater opportunity for both professions to meet, greet, and work together. Sharing what each association is already doing well can help in an initial brainstorming session to connect activities and services and form a community of "best practices." A timely example of this is how AASL has developed its "Standards for the Twenty-First Century Learners" as a teaching model to prepare students for a more knowledge-based, technological world. The twenty-first-century learner will be able to:

1. Inquire, think critically, and gain knowledge;
2. Draw conclusions, make informed decisions, apply knowledge to new situations, and create new knowledge;
3. Share knowledge and participate ethically and productively as members of our democratic society; and
4. Pursue personal and aesthetic growth (AASL 2008).

Unlike formal in-service training events and team-oriented assignments, CoPs can be viewed as informal loosely organized groups that come together to communicate and share both in actual prearranged meetings or settings and through virtual social-networking tools. The key is having a leadership emerge to encourage the loose formation of these various communities. Librarians can be at the forefront of this with an early school year kick-off event such as the aforementioned breakfast summit and can begin to influence the development of this knowledge-sharing venue.

Organizing and hosting a yearly children's literature and reading conference on a regional level offers the potential to forge relationships between many of the players in an educational community. The local university and community college, day care and early childhood agencies, teachers, reading specialists, parents, and anyone with an interest in the subject can attend and begin to consider a continued communication by forming more localized CoPs with a general interest in children's literature where discussion clubs, genres, or literary criticism may be the focus.

Other possible focuses for CoPs include:

Struggling Readers

A group of tutors, librarians, parents, teachers, graduate reading specialist candidates, and mentoring professors can share best practices, strategies, core principles of instruction, and suggested reading materials in leveled units.

Emergent Readers

Day care and early childhood teachers, parents, librarians, and college students can come together to share good, predictable literature choices, read-aloud techniques, picture book extended activities, rhyming and poetry, and retelling opportunities.

Storytelling in and out of the Classroom

The goals of reading instruction can be more subtly achieved through the elements of storytelling. Teachers, librarians, forensics coaches, and local storytelling guild members can come together to establish practices, supporting techniques, and performing opportunities. A yearly festival can be an objective where older children tell or perform for younger kids or even forensics teams flanked by professional raconteurs come together for a weekend or evening of storytelling for the entire community.

Grade Level Curriculum-Specific

PTO/school/library monthly update sessions can be accomplished through liaison meetings and virtual social-networking tools. Assignments, reading strategies, and literature-specific booklists can be incorporated through school and library blogs, wikis, or free online course management systems such as Moodle (http://Moodle.org).

Dovetailing the school's annual fall grade level open house for parents with library initiatives revolving around reading instruction can be orchestrated as the classroom parent, teacher, and library representative join together for an informative kick-off event.

Research and Academic Literacy

As learning to read transitions to reading to learn, subject-oriented teachers, reading specialists, and librarians can share comprehension initiatives to extend reading in content areas.

Visual Literacy

From picture books to graphic novels to online reading practices, new approaches to the reading curriculum will bridge technology, art, and reading instruction.

Student-Related Programming

Reading buddies, homework centers, and tutoring can be better established and coordinated through the leadership and collaboration of the extended educational community beyond the immediate classroom. An example of this might be to create a relationship between education majors required to complete fieldwork, their master professors, and the school community (teachers, parents, and students) requiring tutoring assistance. The library can be a logical location to facilitate the program.

Children's Literature Through Book Discussion and BookTalks

Periodic breakfast, lunch, or even after-work dinners filled with new and established titles to discuss or booktalk for both the pleasure of reading and the curriculum-based connections work to build relationships between school and library personnel.

In essence, CoPs are about relationships that are created and developed between communities of professionals both within their domain and outside it. As with any good relationship, trust and confidence in the sharing and learning of old and new strategies, creating of achievable goals through mutual respect is what makes this order of communication effective. Welcoming ideas from outside your immediate circle and being welcomed for your strengths and knowledge to a former inner circle beyond your own is how communities grow and thrive. And while creating CoPs may seem to add more work to the busy life of teachers and librarians alike, they do not have to be formal or permanent structures or gatherings. A few monthly early before-work coffee shop encounters or after-work early dinners at the local diner or bistro to share and implement a particular idea or strategy can simply be arranged and discontinued as needed.

Face-to-face discussions and meetings can be kept to a minimum with the added advantage of the wide berth of social networking venues available today over the Internet. The recent publication of the American Association of School Librarians Best Web sites for Teaching and Learning (http://www.ala.org/ala/mgrps/divs/aasl/guidelinesandstandards/bestlist/bestwebsites.cfm) offers a terrific place to start with "the Top 25 Web sites [that] foster the qualities of innovation, creativity, active participation, and collaboration. They are free, Web-based sites that are user friendly and encourage a community of learners to explore and discover." Social networking tools such as Classroom2.0 (http://www.classroom20.com/) and Edublogs (http://edublogs.org/) offer virtual CoPs for novice and experienced educators. Good-Reads (http://www.goodreads.com/) is great for online discussion groups concerning young adult and children's literature.

Finding your specific place online can be a good way to get yourself started in a CoP as you begin to branch out beyond your immediate comfort zone within your community of children's librarians.

References

American Association of School Librarians. "Learning 4 Life: A National Plan for Implementation of Standards for the 21st Century Learner and Empowering Learners: Guidelines for School Media Programs." Chicago: American Library Association, 2008, http://www.ala.org/aasl/learning4life.

American Library Association, http://www.ala.org.

Braunger, Jane, and Jan Patricia Lewis. *Building a Knowledge Base in Reading*. Joint publication. Newark, DE: International Reading Association, and Urbana, IL: National Council of Teachers of English, 2006.

Bush, Gail. *The School Buddy System: The Practice of Collaboration*. Chicago: ALA, 2003.

International Reading Association, http://www.reading.org.

Making a Difference Means Making It Different: Honoring Children's Rights to Excellent Reading Instruction, A Position Statement of the International Reading Association. Newark, DE: International Reading Association, 2000.

Wenger, Etienne, Richard McDermott, and William M. Snyder. *Cultivating Communities of Practice: A Guide to Managing Knowledge*. Boston: Harvard Business School Press, 2002.

CHAPTER 7

Keeper of the Tools

When I moved to Michigan and began work as head of youth services in a suburban public library, one of the first things I evaluated was the collection. This was a well-endowed library with a very supportive residential and business tax base in an upper-middle-class town. Reviewing circulation statistics and "reading" the shelves to note where and how the collection had been organized revealed a surprising fact. The fairy tale and folklore collection had one of the lowest circulation records that I had ever seen for such a well-read and educated community. I puzzled over this for a while, wondering why the children and families here seemed to almost ignore the part of the collection that in other communities always circulated right behind the most popular picture books. What made the difference here was where folklore had been shelved, interfiled with the rest of the nonfiction books—at the end of the 300s and just before the 400s. The entire 398 collection with its wonderfully artistic versions, many in picture book format, was hidden between social sciences and language within the taller nonfiction shelves. I decided to do a little rearranging, devoting a special lower shelf unit near the play area and picture books for the 398s. After only three months, circulation statistics for fairy tale and folklore almost tripled! Why? The books were more accessible, in full view, and in close proximity to the much-used and well-loved picture book collection.

The one aspect of reading instruction that all educators, reading theorists, reading specialists, librarians, and parents agree on is that children need numerous opportunities to read, with constant access to books. Access to reading materials beyond the classroom is vital to realizing reading success. The more kids read and the more exposure they are given to reading through various circumstances, the more they gain in their ability to master skills and develop a base for reading with meaning. Jane Braunger and Jan Patricia Lewis assert this theory in their 2006 publication *Building A Knowledge Base in Reading*. Their determined assessment on how to enhance reading instruction outlines the following:

"Readers at all stages of development need access to:

Time for reading and learning.

Texts of all kinds and rich resources for reading.

Knowledgeable and supportive teachers.

Appropriate instruction in skills and strategies.

Demonstrations of how readers, writers, and texts work.

Other readers, both novice and expert.

Their own reading processes" (p. 141).

Librarians are experts in fostering the above access needs through collection development and reading-based programming not only for children and families, but for teachers and school staff. Libraries are the crucial link in the effort to bring an entire educational community together to foster reading development through joint initiatives and committee involvement that promotes a balanced approach to access. If access is the key to providing reading instruction support, the way the collection is acquired, managed, offered, and promoted is key to the way access to reading opportunities is made available for all readers—emergent, new, struggling, and proficient.

Building and maintaining a collection around literacy instruction has primarily been the responsibility of the teacher-librarian or reading specialist. However, the public library is and should be considered an extension of the school and classrooms with the dual ability of providing access to recreational and informational reading that includes a literacy instruction component. And in the twenty-first century, reading instruction involves multiple literacies using media, visual elements, and other forms of technology such as blogs, wikis, and instant messaging that dovetail with traditional book reading.

When you evaluate your collection for literacy instruction, consider three basic principles for better accessibility—visibility, compatibility, and portability.

Collection Development for Literacy Instruction Criteria

Visibility

A children's library can be a welcoming place, yet a bit overwhelming for parents and new or struggling readers in terms of selecting materials. Visibility means merchandising or displaying in ways that bring the collection into direct view for the user. While shelving in strict Dewey order may still work for the majority of your nonfiction collection, what can your youngest new readers find more easily within their newly acquired reading ability among the wealth of books up and down the nonfiction aisles? Highlighting key subject areas such as animal science or pet care, transportation, space vehicles, or rock collecting in separate, monthly small exhibits in close proximity to the picture book and easy-reader collections will draw the eye of a child or parent used to selecting only from the wealth of story choices. But a better way can be to create a more comprehensive nonfiction unit that is just right for these emergent and new eager readers.

Like the folklore collection mentioned above, creating an early nonfiction collection in close proximity to your easy readers is just the thing to bring informational early books to the forefront. I created a discovery section of nonfiction easy-to-read books and housed them in Dewey order right near the easy-reader fiction collection. This way, kindergartners through second graders had an opportunity to select their own books from a smaller, more appropriately leveled section. Many of these early nonfiction books look like picture books or easy readers with their carefully developed text and layouts. You can cull a core collection of easy-to-read nonfiction books across the board, from airplanes to zoology. The goal is not to try to evaluate each title by reading level, but to look for choices that fit into a picture book and easy-reader format.

Sifting through the wealth of nonfiction and determining reading levels can be overwhelming, so an easy way to begin is to select titles from the well-received early and young reading nonfiction series, such as HarperCollins Let's-Read-and-Find-Out and the newer Let's-Read-and-Find-Out Science. Anne Rockwell's recent contributions to this series include the very relevant topics of global warming in *Why are the Ice Caps Melting?* (2006), as well as fossil fuels in *What's So Bad About Gasoline?* (2009). National Geographic has produced a series introducing scientific inquiry with Becky Baines's list of books in the Zigzag series, featuring hibernation in *A Den is a Bed for a Bear* (2008), space science in *Every Planet Has a Place* (2008), and life science in *The Bones You Own* (2009) or *Your Skin Holds You In* (2008). Heinemann has recently published some respectable series in the areas of careers with People in the Community (2008), animal versus human anatomy with Spot the Difference (2008), environmental science with Help the Environment (2008), and transportation with Getting Around (2005). And well-established authors like Vicki Cobb with her award-winning set Science Play, Joanna Cole with her signature and enduring Magic School Bus books, and Gail Gibbons's numerous early nonfiction works all provide good choices for a wealth of intriguing topics in easily read and accessible text. Equally important, these books include wonderful photography, clear drawings, and inspiring artwork.

Take the time to peruse your nonfiction shelves for hot topics that early readers get excited about. Animals in their habitat both wild and domestic are always a favorite. Start with the award-winning photographer Nic Bishop with his two incredibly lifelike exposés on tree frogs, *Red-Eyed Tree Frog* (Scholastic, 1999), and chameleons, *Chameleon, Chameleon* (Scholastic, 2005), both expertly written by Joy Cowley, a master of easy-to-read text.

Good Early Nonfiction Series Choices for a Discovery Collection

Leake, Diyan. People in the Community series (Heinemann Library, 2008)
Titles: *Dentists, Doctors, Firefighters, Police Officers, Teachers, Vets*
Guillain, Charlotte. Help the Environment series (Heinemann Library, 2008)
Titles: *Caring for Nature, Cleaning Up Litter, Reusing and Recycling, Saving Energy, Saving Water*
Nunn, Daniel, and Charlotte Guillain. Spot the Difference series (Heinemann Library, 2008)
Titles: *Ears, Eyes, Noses, Leaves, Roots, Stems*
Mayer, Cassie. Getting Around series (Heinemann Library, 2006)
Titles: *By Bicycle, By Boat, By Car, By Plane, By Train, On Foot*
Cobb, Vicki. Science Play series (HarperCollins)
Titles: *I Face the Wind* (2003), *I Fall Down* (2004), *I Get Wet* (2002), *I See Myself* (2002)

Steve Jenkins and Robin Page use a repetitive text "In the desert I see. . . . In the forest I see . . . ," in which readers look for eight hidden animals in their informative and interactive *I See A Kookaburra!: Discovering Animal Habitats Around the World* (Houghton Mifflin, 2005). *The World That We Want* by Michelle Kim Toft (Charlesbridge, 2005) uses a cumulative pattern to describe how the natural world of animals and their environments are interconnected. Linda Glaser's latest offering in her Classic Creatures series, *Dazzling Dragonflies: A Life Cycle* (Millbrook, 2008), pairs a rhythmic, easy-flowing text with Mia Posada's watercolor and paper collages for a complete look at these daunting insects. Bold, block printing accompanied by crisp photography offers pet information in Angela Royston's Baby Animal series (Chrysalis Education, 2005). Titles include *Puppy*, *Kitten*, *Chick*, *Lamb*, and *Rabbit*. For an interesting and true pet dog story that recounts the New York Philharmonic hall's principal stagehand's unusual experience with the orchestra and his music-loving pet, consider the picture book *Jake the Philharmonic Dog* by Karen LeFrak (Walker, 2006). *Elephants Can Paint Too!* by Katya Arnold (Atheneum, 2005) introduces a unique look at a group of elephants in Asia who have been trained to create paintings as part of the nonprofit organization for the conservation of elephants, the Asian Elephant Art and Conservation Project (AEACP). The dual one-sentence description opposite a longer three- to four-sentence description works for new and more fluent readers simultaneously.

The topic of dinosaurs, always a winning request, has a plethora of choices. Two most suited to a discovery collection feature the classic style of Gail Gibbons in her latest *Dinosaurs!* (Holiday House, 2008), or the fun version in *Dinosaur Bones* by Bob Barner (Chronicle, 2001), sporting an informative and poetic dual text.

Under space and flight, a new publication honoring the fortieth anniversary of the moon landing, *One Giant Leap* by Robert Burleigh (Philomel, 2009), will have a new generation of readers excited as they learn about the event in short, descriptive sentences set against Mike Wimmer's realistic paintings. And *Going Around the Sun: Some Planetary Fun* by Marianne Berkes (Dawn Publications, 2008) incorporates all the planets in our solar system in a rhyming "Over in the Meadow" style repetitive pattern text. Readers will view the planets "whirl, spin, roll, tilt, and blow" around the sun. Carmen Bredeson's I Like Space series includes the simply written *What Do Astronauts Do* (Enslow, 2008).

Move into life sciences with a look at the food chain in *Trout Are Made of Trees* by April Pulley Sayre (Charlesbridge, 2008), featuring a collage-style set of illustrations to enhance a lyrical and basic one- to two-sentence per page ecological story. Balance this with Sayre's unique topic on dust and all its forms in her book *Stars Beneath Your Bed* (Greenwillow, 2005), with Ann Jonas's signature block-style illustrations. The dispersal of seeds is beautifully represented in a mellifluous yet facile text in *Flip, Float, Fly: Seeds on the Move* by JoAnn Early Macken (Holiday House, 2008), with clear, deep acrylics by Pam Paparone. All three of these picture book style publications could be missed in a general nonfiction collection by the audience for whom they are intended.

Seasons and weather have an old standby choice by Catherine and Laurence Anholt, *Sun Snow Stars Sky* (Penguin, 1995), providing an easy-to-read tour of the changing seasons. Shelley Rotner's photo essay *Every Season* (Roaring Brook Press, 2007) with its collection of short seasonal statements gives new readers a realistic and relatable experience.

A hands-on learning book filled with activities easily replicable at home and at school is one that features construction concepts, *Let's Try It Out with Towers and Bridges* by veteran science writer Seymour Simon (Simon & Schuster, 2003). *C is for Caboose* by Traci N. Todd (Chronicle Books, 2007) not only outlines train transportation in an alphabetic picture book format complimented by basic sentences, it also interweaves American history with the railroad's development in a montage of photographic and bold period-style drawings by Steve Vance. And Brian Floca in *Lightship* (Atheneum, 2007) introduces the functionality and purpose of a lightship with his clear, simply drawn watercolors matched with a large block print set in an easy-reader format modeled after the original Harper & Row series.

From these hot subjects, move into other less frequented areas by early and new readers such as time with *A Second is a Hiccup* by Hazel Hutchins (Arthur A. Levine, 2007) or math with a selection of Stuart Murphy's MathStart series (HarperCollins) that introduce varying concepts from patterns, to addition, to sequencing and making predictions.

Include Mathematic Concepts in Your Discovery Collection

MathStart books (HarperCollins) by Stuart Murphy
Beep Beep, Vroom Vroom! (2000)
Jack the Builder (2006)
Mall Mania (2006)
Same Old Horse (2005)

Fractions are cleverly tackled in *Full House* by Dayle Ann Dodds (Candlewick Press, 2007), while easy-to-read word problems are keenly crafted in *You Can, Toucan, Math* by David Adler (Holiday House, 2006) and *Math Appeal: Mind-Stretching Math Riddles* by Greg Tang (Scholastic, 2003).

Remember to include the range of nonfiction right through biography. David Adler's signature series A Picture Book of . . . concentrates on many of America's historical figures with the latest on James Madison and his wife—*A Picture Book of Dolley and James Madison* (Holiday House, 2009). Picture book biographies have been around for several years now, targeted at older readers, yet Robert Burleigh succeeds in creating two sports figure books with short poetic sentences that early readers will appreciate. *By My Brother's Side* (Simon & Schuster, 2004) highlights football stars and twin brothers Tiki and Ronde Barber, while *Home Run* (Harcourt Brace, 1998) is an homage to Babe Ruth. Picture book to easy-reader format can be included in a discovery collection for the same figures, such as Anne Rockwell's *Big George: How a Shy Boy Became President Washington* (Harcourt, 2009) with Matt Phelan's soft pencil and gouache paintings, or David Adler's Holiday House easy reader *President George Washington* (2005) with lively watercolors by John Wallner. Offering a plethora of nonfiction titles in a more accessible way will not only improve circulation of these books, but they will be read many more times by the readers they attract, new, early fluent, and transitional. And in the best of worlds, if budgets permit, having duplicates in the regular nonfiction area will enhance your accessibility.

Other sections can be created for alphabet books, numbering, and size perception—the traditional concept books. Pulling them from the regular picture book section and placing them in their own space makes it easier for parents to hone in on the plethora of pre-reading concepts young children master before and after starting school. These separate collections can also be augmented with the use of pathfinders and content-based bibliographies highlighting titles, series, and authors to benefit your emergent, new, and struggling readers. All this rearranging may send your technical services and cataloging department into a tizzy, so work with them to create some coding unique to your department. It is well worth the effort to help your young readers access the materials they need to develop their skills and reading interests.

Compatibility

Recurring assignments and familiar reference questions are staples when evaluating reviews and other resources to acquire new items for your collection. Equally important are the basic goals of reading instruction which aim to:

- Establish a sense of enjoyment.
- Create an understanding of ownership and independence.
- Develop skills and strategies.
- Develop fluency.
- Construct meaning.
- Synthesize and evaluate content.

As students work their way through the reading instruction process, difficulties can hamper their overall sense of pleasurable reading experiences. Compatibility refers to how a reader can successfully achieve the above instructional goals while reading both assignment and personal-interest materials that fall within his or her independent and instructional levels. Make it easy to supplement assignments with materials that can be compatible with the instructional goals of the child's classroom, and take the tension away from a rigid reading program. Provide opportunities through the available selection of visual and media materials to supplement classroom literacy strategies. From graphic novels to compact discs to computer games, these forms of media literacy help to establish how print and non-print work together for meaningful content.

The library visit is generally a way for the child to establish a sense of enjoyment when given the opportunity to select from a larger sphere of literacy materials of his or her interest that helps him or her gain a sense of ownership and independence. A recent *New York Times* article, "Students Get New Reading Assignment: Pick Books You Like" (August 30, 2009, p. 1), focused on the Reading Workshop classroom environment that replaces some or much of the traditional required reading lists on the curriculum with students' own reading choices as a motivator for higher interest with increased reading achievement. Create revolving displays of collections such as predictable books that supplement some of the early strategies in a kindergarten classroom. Offer pathfinders or bibliographies listing easy rhyming trade books that are perfect for phonics development. Titles such as Eve B. Feldman's latest, *Billy & Milly, Short & Silly* (Putnam Juvenile, 2009), incorporate brilliant one-word noun/verb combinations to reflect several short scenarios in rhyming and phonetic patterns.

Just-Emerging Readers

Capucilli, Alyssa Satin. Biscuit series (HarperCollins)

Gorbachev, Valeri. *Whose Hat is It?* (HarperCollins, 2004)

Grant, Judyann Ackerman. *Chicken Said, "Cluck!"* (HarperCollins, 2008)

Willems, Mo. *Pigs Make Me Sneeze* (Hyperion, 2009)

Pig Wig (Blue Apple, 2006) and *Snake Cake* (Blue Apple, 2006), both by Yukiko Kido, are great examples of wordplay and creating word families.

Evaluate your easy-reader collection and rather than creating a detailed leveling system, organize it into three larger subcategories for just-emerging readers, new readers, and fluent and independent readers. This way, many of your titles will be compatible with the way the school's literacy collections are organized and allow for more independent selection by your patrons, with a clearer understanding by parents of the leveled ranges offered in the school. Spine color-coding for each subcategory with a handout and signage offering a brief guide to each color will make this organization clear to parents and teachers. HarperCollins' My First I Can Read series as well as Mo Willems with his Elephant and Piggie books (Hyperion) are perfect examples of short, well-designed first choices.

New readers can easily work with many of the standard trade easy reader's from a variety of publishers. From Denys Cazet's Minnie and Moo collection to the classic Syd Hoff choices, this is the area to include short, well-spaced multiple sentences on one page. Very early three- to four-chapter sections such as those offered in Lobel's Frog and Toad books are appropriate here.

Early chapter books with larger fonts and several short chapters can be offered in the fluent and independent readers section as a gradual transition to the larger, more complete, and multileveled

New Readers

Marshall, James. *Fox at School.* Dial, 1993, and others.

McCully, Emily Arnold. *Grandmas at Bat.* HarperCollins, 1993, and others.

Rylant, Cynthia. *Henry and Mudge and the Big Sleepover.* Simon & Schuster, 2006, and others.

Fluent and Independent Readers

Blume, Judy. *Going, Going, Gone! with the Pain and the Great One* (Delacorte, 2008)
Friend or Fiend with the Pain and the Great One (Delacorte, 2009)
Gregorich, Barbara. *Waltur Buys a Pig in a Poke and Other Stories* (Houghton Mifflin, 2006)
Waltur Paints Himself in a Corner (Houghton Mifflin, 2007)
Lowry, Lois. *Gooney Bird Greene* (Houghton Mifflin, 2002)
McDonald, Megan. *Stink: The Incredible Shrinking Kid* (Candlewick, 2005)

---

fiction collection. Books such as the new Mercy Watson series by Kate DiCamillo (Candlewick), the Owen Foote series by Stephanie Greene (Clarion), or even the classic Nora, Teddy, Russell, and Elisa stories by Johanna Hurwitz, repackaged as the Riverside Kids series by HarperCollins, work well here.

Finally, be cognizant of helping students and parents with comprehension by offering discussable books on all levels with key or provocative content that children can think about, retell, and interpret. Choose books with great character-study potential to fuel discussion that encourages literary interpretation and meaningful reading. Analyzing feelings and thoughts in a character like Kevin Henkes's *Chrysanthemum* (Greenwillow, 1991) or William Steig's *Shrek* (Farrar, Straus, and Giroux, 1990), or the very opposite Chinese American figures of Jin Wang and Danny in the graphic novel *American Born Chinese* by Gene Luen Yang (First Second, 2006), or the quirky character of the Dybbuk in Sid Fleischman's satirical portrayal of the Holocaust in *The Entertainer and the Dybbuk* (Greenwillow, 2008) offers children at various reading and listening levels the opportunity to delve deeper into the author's purpose through his or her words.

Portability

Reading instruction beyond the classroom setting is dependent on the key players in the surrounding educational community. Portability refers to the ability to bring the collection to these players outside the library walls to allow for easier access and a greater understanding of what your library provides. Providing access to your collection through portable opportunities makes the collection available to tutors, college and university faculty and students, local literacy councils, community-service organizations, day care centers, and parent-groups actively interested in promoting reading. Offer tutoring kits, units by levels or subject matter, story time plans, or simply an on-demand service for teachers and tutors with preselected books and materials by request. To expand on the reading experience, consider purchasing some prepackaged story and activity kits from a commercial educational vendor such as Childcraft; these can include a classic picture book, manipulatives, and activity sheets filled with extensions related to the concept or theme. These kits are quite effective with struggling and special-needs students requiring the extra tactile component to aid comprehension. Tutors and parents will welcome these additions to a portable, circulating collection. By the same token, you can create some nonfiction kits using some of the science, math, music, or art titles from a discovery collection combined with suggested activities or easy projects for teachers to use as an extension to their curriculum.

You can also extend the portability of your collection through your library's Web site by including links for reading instruction tips and guidelines, bibliographies, and actual Web resources such as those highlighted by ALSC's Great Web sites for Kids. Web sites such as Reading Rockets (http://www.readingrockets.org/) produced by PBS or RIF's Leading to Reading (http://www.rif.org/kids/leadingtoreading/en/leadingtoreading.htm) provide stories and activities geared toward reading instruction. Links to other children's digital libraries such as the award-winning The Story Place produced by the Public Library of Charlotte and Mecklenburg County in North Carolina (http://www.storyplace.org/) or the International Children's Digital Library (http://en.childrenslibrary.org/) are other ways to extend your collection beyond your library's walls. Digital children's books are already on the horizon, with publishers offering online opportunities to read via the screen. From subscription services like the TumbleBooks Library (http://www.tumblebooklibrary.com) to online magazines like Babybug offered through *Cricket* magazine (http://www.cricketmag.com), these choices complement the newer features with classic children's selections that many moms and dads have available now through their iPhone kids e-book reader application or through e-readers such as Amazon's Kindle.

Promotion, Promotion, Promotion

Finally, as with anything you do to bring about awareness of the library's services, promotion through outreach meetings, advertising, communities of practice, and online library blogs or wikis are essential in letting your reading instruction community, children, and parents realize the potential a library's collection has for providing access to reading opportunities.

One effective and fairly inexpensive way is to develop an online periodic newsletter for your surrounding educational community, a kind of gateway to the library's role in supporting reading instruction. Promote it through either an e-mail sign-up, as many publisher and review journals do, or with Really Simple Syndication (RSS) feeds. Many of the social networking sites and blogs operate and distribute their content with RSS feeds. Having a blog or wiki as part of your library's Web site is only effective if people log in to read it. Offering a newsletter that comes periodically to a subscriber may be more effective advertising and promotion of your services. Include information about new books and materials to your collection, related literature-based programming, open house parent-teacher nights, and any of the CoP's future work, goals, or accomplishments with invitations to participate. And remember to include an RSS feed link on your Web site to alert users to its existence.

Resources

Barstow, Barbara, Judith Riggle, and Leslie Molnar. *Beyond Picture Books: Subject Access to Best Books for Beginning Readers*. Westport, CT: Libraries Unlimited, 2008.

Braunger, Jane, and Jan Patricia Lewis. *Building a Knowledge Base in Reading*. Joint publication. Newark, DE: International Reading Association, and Urbana, IL: National Council of Teachers of English, 2006.

Rich, Motoko. "Students Get New Reading Assignment: Pick Books You Like." *New York Times*, August 30, 2009.

Children's Books Cited

Adler, David. *A Picture Book of Dolley and James Madison*. New York: Holiday House, 2009.
Adler, David. *President George Washington*. New York: Holiday House, 2005.
Adler, David. *You Can, Toucan, Math*. New York: Holiday House, 2006.

Anholt, Catherine, and Laurence Anholt. *Sun Snow Stars Sky*. New York: Penguin, 1995.

Arnold, Katya. *Elephants Can Paint Too!* New York: Atheneum, 2005.

Baines, Becky. *A Den is a Bed for a Bear*. Washington, D.C.: National Geographic, 2008.

Baines, Becky. *The Bones You Own*. Washington, D. C.: National Geographic, 2009.

Baines, Becky. *Every Planet Has a Place*. Washington, D. C.: National Geographic, 2008.

Baines, Becky. *Your Skin Holds You In*. Washington, D. C.: National Geographic, 2008.

Barner, Bob. *Dinosaur Bones*. San Francisco: Chronicle, 2001.

Berkes, Marianne. *Going Around the Sun: Some Planetary Fun*. Nevada City, CA: Dawn Publications, 2008.

Bishop, Nic, and Joy Cowley. *Chameleon, Chameleon*. New York: Scholastic, 2005.

Bishop, Nic, and Joy Cowley. *Red-Eyed Tree Frog*. New York: Scholastic, 1999.

Blume, Judy. *Friend or Fiend with the Pain and the Great One*. New York: Delacorte, 2009.

Blume, Judy. *Going, Going, Gone! with the Pain and the Great One*. New York: Delacorte, 2008.

Bredeson, Carmen. *What Do Astronauts Do*. Berkeley Heights, NJ: Enslow, 2008.

Burleigh, Robert. *By My Brother's Side*. New York: Simon & Schuster, 2004.

Burleigh, Robert. *Home Run*. New York: Harcourt Brace, 1998.

Burleigh, Robert. *One Giant Leap*. New York: Philomel, 2009.

Capucilli, Alyssa Satin. Biscuit series. New York: HarperCollins.
Titles: *Biscuit* (1996), *Biscuit's picnic* 1998), *Hello Biscuit* (1998), *Biscuit wants to play* (2001), *Biscuit goes to the park* (2001), *Biscuit visits the doctor* (2008)

Cobb, Vicki. Science Play series. New York: HarperCollins.
Titles: *I Face the Wind* (2003), *I Fall Down* (2004), *I Get Wet* (2002), *I See Myself* (2002)

Dodds, Dayle Ann. *Full House*. Cambridge, MA: Candlewick Press, 2007.

Feldman, Eve B. *Billy & Milly, Short & Silly*. New York: Putnam Juvenile, 2009.

Fleischman, Sid. *The Entertainer and the Dybbuk*. New York: Greenwillow, 2008.

Floca, Brian. *Lightship*. New York: Atheneum, 2007.

Gibbons, Gail. *Dinosaurs!*. New York: Holiday House, 2008.

Glaser, Linda. *Dazzling Dragonflies: A Life Cycle*. Minneapolis: Millbrook, 2008.

Gorbachev, Valeri. *Whose Hat is It?* New York: HarperCollins, 2004.

Grant, Judyann Ackerman. *Chicken Said, "Cluck!"* New York: HarperCollins, 2008.

Gregorich, Barbara. *Waltur Buys a Pig in a Poke and Other Stories.* New York: Houghton Mifflin, 2006.

Gregorich, Barbara. *Waltur Paints Himself in a Corner.* New York: Houghton Mifflin, 2007.

Guillain, Charlotte. Help the Environment series. Chicago: Heinemann Library, 2008.

Titles: *Caring for Nature, Cleaning Up Litter, Reusing and Recycling, Saving Energy, Saving Water*

Henkes, Kevin. *Chrysanthemum.* New York: Greenwillow, 1991.

Hutchins, Hazel. *A Second is a Hiccup.* New York: Arthur A. Levine, 2007.

Jenkins, Steve, and Robin Page. *I See A Kookaburra!: Discovering Animal Habitats Around the World.* New York: Houghton Mifflin, 2005.

Kido, Yukiko. *Pig Wig.* New York: Blue Apple, 2006.

Kido, Yukiko. *Snake Cake.* New York: Blue Apple, 2006.

Leake, Diyan. People in the Community series. Chicago: Heinemann Library, 2008.

Titles: *Dentists, Doctors, Firefighters, Police Officers, Teachers, Vets*

LeFrak, Karen. *Jake the Philharmonic Dog.* New York: Walker, 2006.

Lowry, Lois. *Gooney Bird Greene.* New York: Houghton Mifflin, 2002.

Macken, JoAnn Early. *Flip, Float, Fly Seeds on the Move.* New York: Holiday House, 2008.

Marshall, James. *Fox at School.* New York: Dial, 1993.

Mayer, Cassie. Getting Around series. Chicago: Heinemann Library, 2006.

Titles: *Getting Around by Bicycle, Getting Around by Boat, Getting Around by Car, Getting Around by Plane, Getting Around by Train, Getting Around on Foot*

Nunn, Daniel, and Charlotte Guillain. Spot the Difference series. Chicago: Heinemann Library, 2008.

Titles: *Ears, Eyes, Noses, Leaves, Roots, Stems*

McCully, Emily Arnold. *Grandmas at Bat.* New York: HarperCollins, 1993.

McDonald, Megan. *Stink: The Incredible Shrinking Kid.* Cambridge, MA: Candlewick, 2005.

Murphy, Stuart. *Beep Beep, Vroom Vroom!.* New York: HarperCollins, 2000.

Murphy, Stuart. *Jack the Builder.* New York: HarperCollins, 2006.

Murphy, Stuart. *Mall Mania.* New York: HarperCollins, 2006.

Murphy, Stuart. *Same Old Horse.* New York: HarperCollins, 2005.

Rockwell, Anne. *Big George: How a Shy Boy Became President Washington*. New York: Harcourt, 2009.

Rockwell, Anne. *What's So Bad About Gasoline?* New York: HarperCollins, 2009.

Rockwell, Anne. *Why Are the Ice Caps Melting?* New York: HarperCollins, 2006.

Rotner, Shelley. *Every Season*. New Milford, CT: Roaring Brook Press, 2007.

Royston, Angela. Baby Animal series. North Mankato, MN: Chrysalis Education, 2005.

Titles: *Puppy, Kitten, Chick, Lamb, Rabbit*

Rylant, Cynthia. *Henry and Mudge and the Big Sleepover*. New York: Simon & Schuster, 2006.

Sayre, April Pulley. *Stars Beneath Your Bed*. New York: Greenwillow, 2005.

Sayre, April Pulley. *Trout Are Made of Trees*. Watertown, MA: Charlesbridge, 2008.

Simon, Seymour. *Let's Try It Out with Towers and Bridges*. New York: Simon & Schuster, 2003.

Steig, William. *Shrek*. New York: Farrar, Straus, and Giroux, 1990.

Tang, Greg. *Math Appeal: Mind-Stretching Math Riddles*. New York: Scholastic, 2003.

Todd, Traci N. *C is for Caboose*. San Francisco: Chronicle Books, 2007.

Toft, Michelle Kim. *The World That We Want*. Watertown, MA: Charlesbridge, 2005.

Willems, Mo. *Pigs Make Me Sneeze*. New York: Hyperion, 2009.

Yang, Gene Luen. *American Born Chinese*. New York: First Second, 2006.

CHAPTER 8

Insights

One of the most important conclusions that can be gathered from the research and instructional methods practiced over the last seventy-five years is that children really do not learn to read in early elementary school and thereafter read to learn. In a recent article summing up a history of reading philosophy and pedagogy, Australian educator Jan Turbill states, "we are lifelong learners of reading—or, to be more precise, of literacy. We accept that we will learn new skills in new contexts. It is a K–adult curriculum now" (Turbill 2002, 12). Reading skills are developed, practiced, honed, and constantly improved upon throughout a child's life and through adulthood. Reading is not just a skill, but a way of communicating and interpreting information, literary knowledge, language, and linguistic appreciation through the varied sources of print and visual literacies offered by the publishing world. This requires a very delicate balance between the teaching of good problem-solving strategies that foster an awareness of the basic skills and how to apply them with a continued cultivation of children's interests, enthusiasm for learning, and willingness to keep trying, to persevere, in order to achieve.

What we have learned from some of the more innovative programs over the last twenty years, such as Reading Recovery, is that struggling readers need to be helped one child at a time in models that offer intervention as early as kindergarten and first grade. However, five basic underlying principles of Reading Recovery can and should be incorporated through all areas of education. Cox and Hopkins state this in their 2006 article:

- Reading is a complex problem-solving process.
- Children construct their own understandings of the reading process.
- Children come to literacy with varying knowledge.
- Reading and writing are reciprocal and interrelated processes.
- Children take different paths to literacy learning.

While Reading Recovery is meant for struggling readers trying to achieve basic literacy, the above underlying principles provide insight for children's librarians in the role of reading advocate to include a wider range of experiences and activities for a broad spectrum of children's interests and experiences through readers' advisory, reference, and programming opportunities.

Literacy is a struggle in this country not only for children, but for adults as well. Librarians have worked to support the educational community through various family literacy programs. As with Reading Recovery that involves parental participation each night, public library programming such as Every Child Ready to Read @ Your Library and Prime Time Reading include the third important component of a successful education model, the involved parent. The parent/child discussion model must be encouraged throughout the grades as transitional readers develop their advanced strategies for successful reading.

Librarians can encourage teachers to be more avid readers of children's books in order to be able to move each child through the process of learning to read and reading to learn effectively. Teaching is about modeling. In-school or after-school teacher-to-teacher book clubs foster teacher-to-student and student-to-student book discussion. Literature-based teacher staff development, in addition to reading instruction communities of practice, must be incorporated within an educational community to create a complete circle of reading instruction support in and outside the school and library settings.

Tailoring collections to provide the all-important and crucial access that each reader and supporter of reading instruction needs through the visibility of organized, easily retrieved units or sections, the compatibility of assignments and classroom literacy libraries, and the portability of on-demand enrichment kits and virtual reading occasions link public libraries to the internal world of reading education.

Keeping up with Trends

New ideas, methods, or theories are always on the horizon, and keeping up is a good idea to completely offer service that is current and complementary with the times. The following annotated list of associations, journals, books, and other Web resources can help you stay in the loop. Also, networking with teachers and teacher-librarians is a good way to stay apprised of new developments.

Associations

The International Reading Association (http://www.reading. org/) offers a wealth of information for teachers, tutors, and parents. The group holds national and regional annual conferences, offers numerous peer-reviewed books for sale, and has an online library for reading research and education-related information. Check for your individual state's Reading Association under Affiliates and Councils of North America (http://www. reading.org/General/LocalAssociations/NorthAmerica.aspx).

The Reading Recovery Council of North America (http://www. readingrecovery.org/) offers a range of programs and services, publications, conferences, advocacy, technical assistance, and special institutes related to the implementation of Reading Recovery. It is a good way to collaborate with early literacy advocates and other education professionals interested in early literacy and early intervention.

The National Council of Teachers of English (http://www.ncte. org/) offers everything related to the teaching of all the language arts, including publications, professional development, Web seminars, and online teaching resources and blogs.

Read Write Think (http://www.readwritethink.org/index.asp) is a partnership between the International Reading Association (IRA), the National Council of Teachers of English (NCTE), and the Verizon Foundation. NCTE and IRA are working together to provide educators and students with access to the highest quality practices and resources in reading and language-arts instruction through free, Internet-based content.

Journals

The Reading Teacher, published by the International Reading Association, is a peer-reviewed journal offering insights into classroom strategies, the latest research information, and reviews of children's literature suitable for literacy instruction.

Reading Today is the IRA's monthly newspaper available to members. It has updated information about critical issues in literacy education, trends influencing the field, classroom strategies, technology, advocacy, and announcements of IRA programs and events. It is a great way to stay connected with the reading specialist and educator profession.

Reading Online (http://www.readingonline.org) is the electronic journal of the IRA, freely available and searchable by author, title, and subject indexes. It includes hundreds of articles from May 1997 to June 2005 on literacy practices for students five to eighteen years of age. "Literacy" is defined as traditional print, visual, critical, media, and digital.

Books

Atwell, Nancie. *Side by Side: Essays on Teaching to Learn.* Portsmouth, NH: Heinemann, 1991.

Drawing on her years of experience teaching reading and writing, Atwell addresses the need for programs that encourage students to work closely with their teachers in ways that encourage reader response and other literate behaviors.

Fountas, Irene C., and Gay Su Pinnell. *The Fountas and Pinnell Leveled Books K–8+: 2010–2012 Edition.* Portsmouth, NH: Heinemann, 2009.

This is an excellent reference resource for understanding the sometimes-confusing and different leveling criteria offered by publishers and educational basal readers. More than 35,000 titles are represented by levels and arranged by title, including classic and contemporary trade books and series-spanning choices by genres for kindergarten through middle school readers.

Fox, Mem. *Radical Reflections: Passionate Opinions on Teaching Learning, and Living.* San Diego: Harcourt, 1993.

With anecdotal reflections, Fox, a former professor in literacy education and an acclaimed children's author, provides insight into the methods of teaching reading as she argues against the "skills and drills" philosophy, advocating for a complete language-arts program that focuses more on children's response to reading and writing.

Fry, Edward B., and Jacqueline E. Kress. *The Reading Teacher's Book of Lists*. Fifth Edition. San Francisco: Jossey-Bass, 2006.

This is a complete resource for teaching reading methods, including 218 lists teachers use to develop phonics, fluency, comprehension, content words, and even children's books that enhance specific strategies.

Keene, Ellin Oliver, and Susan Zimmermann. *Mosaic of Thought*. Portsmouth, NH: Heinemann, 1997.

This is a groundbreaking approach to the reading process and in particular reading comprehension which analyzes and explores how readers use metacognitive strategies to enhance reading proficiency and understanding.

Miller, Debbie. *Reading with Meaning: Teaching Comprehension in the Primary Grades*. Portland, ME: Stenhouse, 2002.

This is an inside look into a primary grade classroom where reading is taught through the techniques of modeling strategic reading through thinking strategies and discussion.

Roser, Nancy L., and Miriam G. Martinez, eds. *What a Character!: Character Study as a Guide to Literary Meaning Making in Grades K–8*. Newark, DE: International Reading Association, 2005.

A diverse group of established children's authors, researchers, and teachers discuss "character" as a literary element, important for the teaching of reading comprehension through discussion.

Szymusiak, Karen, Franki Sibberson, and Lisa Koch. *Beyond Leveled Books: Supporting Early and Transitional Readers in Grades K–5*, 2nd edition. Portland, ME: Stenhouse, 2008.

This is an updated edition with an approach to teaching reading that challenges the leveled-book concept and provides resources and teaching strategies using trade literature for new and transitional readers.

Zimmermann, Susan, and Chryse Hutchins. *7 Keys to Comprehension: How to Help Your Kids Read It and Get It!* New York: Three Rivers Press, 2003.

This offers practical advice using proven steps to help children understand and engage in their reading experiences.

Web Resources

Reading Rockets (http://www.readingrockets.org/) is an educational initiative of WETA, the flagship public television and radio station in the nation's capital, and is funded by a major grant from the U.S. Department of Education, Office of Special Education Programs. It provides a wealth of literacy education information including the following two blogs: http://www.readingrockets.org/blogs.

Sound It Out provides guidance for parents and teachers on the best practices for reading.

Page By Page explores ways to use children's books both inside and outside the classroom.

The National Council for Family Literacy (http://www.famlit.org/) is a national resource with information for philanthropists, educators, parents, and community leaders on bringing literacy into the everyday lives of families. A national conference and a blog (http://www.famlit.org/blog) are among many of the resources available.

PBS Teachers (http://www.pbs.org/teachers/) offers a wide range of free resources for teaching and learning. PBS Kids Raising Readers (http://pbskids.org/read/teachers/) concentrates on lesson plans, tips and tools, and professional development.

As children's librarians, I would like to think that we teach creative reading as Katherine Paterson (1995) describes in her essay, "Reading and Writing,"

> . . . the gift of creative reading, like all natural gifts, must be nourished or it will atrophy . . . in much the same way you nourish the gift of writing—you read, think, talk, look, listen, hate, fear, love, weep—and bring all of your life like a sieve to what you read. (pp. 36–37)

Start the new school year with this in mind. Successful, interested readers make for successful, productive students and adults. This is a worthy goal all administrators, teachers, librarians, and parents must continually work together to achieve.

Resources

Cox, Beverly E., and Carol J. Hopkins "Building on Theoretical Principles Gleaned from Reading Recovery to Inform Classroom Practice." *Reading Research Quarterly* 41 (2) (April/May/June 2006): 254–267.

Paterson, Katherine. *A Sense of Wonder: On Reading and Writing Books for Children.* New York: Penguin Books, 1995.

Turbill, Jan. "The Four Ages of Reading Philosophy and Pedagogy: A Framework for Examining Theory and Practice." *Reading Online* 5 (6) (February 2002), http://www.readingonline.org/international/inter_index.asp?HREF=turbill4/index.html.

Glossary of Reading Instruction Terms

Adequate yearly progress (AYP) Under the No Child Left Behind Act (2001), mandated annual assessments determined by individual states are used to record improvement toward the goal of 100 percent of students achieving some level of improvement in reading/language arts and math each year.

Aesthetic response The emotional connection a reader makes with the text.

Analytic phonics Reading instruction that incorporates phonetic study of words already mastered through the sight word method.

Balanced literacy A philosophy that favors the use of phonics within the context of reading and writing, incorporating basal, trade books, and language experience activities with opportunities to engage children in literacy behaviors through play, performance, and their own writing experiences.

Cloze activity Children fill in the blank as they listen and are able to complete the verses themselves by supplying the order and sequence of the rhyming words.

Constructivist teaching or perspective Learning takes place through an active participant environment in which learners use their prior knowledge, the information presented, and their thinking skills combined.

Cuneiform writing Originating in Mesopotamia, the use of symbols to represent specific sounds.

Efferent Response The meaning or understanding a reader develops from the text.

Fluency Having enough word recognition to read competently with a certain speed, accuracy, intonation, and phrasing.

Frustration reading level A less than 70 percent on an IRI score indicates a reader is frustrated and cannot improve because of a low comprehension level and very little word recognition to facilitate fluency.

Independent reading level A 90–100 percent score on an IRI indicates a reader is comfortable with adequate comprehension, with virtually no errors, and uses self-correction strategies competently. Reader is comfortable, fluent, and shows excellent comprehension.

Informal reading inventory (IRI) An informal assessment of a child's reading and listening levels. Within grade levels, children are evaluated as they place into independent, instructional, frustration, and listening levels.

Instructional reading level A 70–89 percent score on an IRI indicates a reader can be instructed to use corrective strategies effectively. The reader is challenged and remains interested but not frustrated.

Language arts The combined study of reading, writing, speaking, and listening.

Language experience activity The child's personal story or experience written either by the child or a teacher, parent, or tutor, that the child can then reread multiple times on his own to develop word recognition and fluency.

Leveling A progression of small steps, moving from very easy text to more complex reading situations.

Listening level The highest level at which a student can understand material that is read to him and represents an indication of the student's reading potential. Often the listening level will be higher than the reading level.

Metacognition The awareness and monitoring of one's own learning.

Onset The consonant at the beginning of a one-syllable word.

Orthography The learning of the alphabet, decoding sounds, words, and spelling.

Phoneme The smallest unit of a sound in a word.

Phonemic awareness The ability to orally divide speech sounds within words.

Phonological awareness The three sounds that make up all words: syllables, onsets/rimes, and phonemes.

Rime The vowel and consonant(s) that follow an onset or initial consonant.

Scaffolding A teaching method in which teachers use supportive instruction to model certain strategies and then gradually withdraw support as the learner demonstrates the skill being taught.

Syllable A word or part of a word incorporating one unit of sound with one vowel or one vowel with several consonants.

Synthetic phonics The teaching of letters, sounds, and their combination into blends before word recognition is achieved.

Whole language A philosophy that integrates the basic skills of reading with the simultaneous application of all the language arts: speaking, listening, reading, and writing.

Word recognition The ability to identify words easily, whether in context of a sentence or in isolation on a list.

Zone of proximal development A theory based on the work of Russian educational psychologist Lev Vygotsky in which learning potential is greater when placed within a student's ability and prior knowledge subsequently supported by appropriate teacher scaffolding and modeling.

Index

Author has used boldface to indicate main discussion of topics.

About the Author

RITA SOLTAN is the author of *Reading Raps: A Book Club Guide for Librarians, Kids and Families* (Libraries Unlimited, 2005), and *Summer Reading Renaissance: An Interactive Exhibits Approach* (Libraries Unlimited, 2008). She worked as a public children's librarian for thirty-two years in New York and Michigan and supervised youth services departments for fifteen years. Rita holds a BA in Spanish literature/education and an MLS, both from Queens College of the City University of New York. She recently completed an MAT in reading and language arts at Oakland University in Rochester, Michigan. She is currently an independent library youth services consultant and reviews children's books for *Kirkus Reviews*, *Horn Book Guide*, and *School Library Journal*. She also teaches English and library technician courses at Oakland Community College in southeast Michigan. Helping children read and become lovers of books is a goal she pursues throughout her professional life. Visit Rita at her Web site at http://www.ritasoltan.com.